The Rise of Egyptian Communism, 1939–1970

CONTEMPORARY ISSUES IN THE MIDDLE EAST

The Rise of
Egyptian
Communism,
1939–1970

Selma Botman

Syracuse University Press

First Edition
93 92 91 90 89 88   6 5 4 3 2 1

The paper used in this publication meets the minimum requirements of American National Standard for Information Sciences — Permanence of Paper for Printed Library Materials, ANSI Z39.48-1984. ∞™

Library of Congress Cataloging-in-Publication Data

Botman, Selma.
  The rise of Egyptian communism, 1939–1970.

  (Contemporary issues in the Middle East)
  Bibliography: p.
  Includes index.
  1. Communism—Egypt—History. I. Title. II. Series.
HX443.A6B67 1988   320.5'32'0962   88-4916
ISBN 0-8156-2443-3 (alk. paper)

for TOM, who saw this book through
and
for JACK, who so much would have liked to

SELMA BOTMAN is Assistant Professor in the Department of Political Science at the College of the Holy Cross in Worcester, Mass., and is a recipient of several fellowships including the National Endowment for the Humanities and the Social Science Research Council. She received both her M.A. and her Ph.D. from Harvard University and has published articles in a number of scholarly journals.

Contents

Preface

THE MAJORITY OF STUDIES written about the political history of modern Egypt have focused either on parties or movements which have succeeded in assuming power or those whose message inspired considerable numbers of people. Similarly, the figures who have drawn the attention of historians have generally been those able to operate openly in the political arena. This study of Egyptian communism from 1939 to 1970 does not belong to these categories. The Egyptian communist movement never became a mainstream party or even a consistently powerful political force. Instead, it operated in an environment of extreme clandestinity and periodic repression. Its leaders have received little recognition because they were never able to create a mass movement with realistic capabilities for replacing either the royalist regime or Nasserist rule.

Yet, the influence of Egyptian communism was larger than its numbers imply. Communism had a significant ideological impact on Egyptian society, especially on intellectuals and among small groups of skilled workers. Communists were present at key moments of nationalist, student, and trade union militancy, and they contributed to the destabilization of the constitutional regime and the worn-out Wafd Party. In doing so, they helped pave the way for the emergence of Gamal Abdul Nasser and the Free Officers Movement of 1952.

Despite the significance of communism as an intellectual, cultural, and political extra-parliamentary force, its history is virtually unknown. This book addresses that gap by examining the rise and experience of communism within Egyptian society subject to the pressures of the international system. It is offered as a modest contribution to the study of Egypt's political and intellectual history and to the literature of Third World revolutionary movements.

ix

Many people have contributed to this book and to all of them—too numerous to name—I owe a debt of gratitude. I deeply thank all those who granted me interviews and provided me an invaluable record of Egypt in the 1940s, 1950s, and 1960s. Their generosity, interest, and experience made this study possible.

Mahmud Amin al-Alim, Muhammad Sid Ahmad, Fuad Mursi, Albert Arie, Hilmi Yassin, and Soraya Adham gave me their time and encouragement and shared with me their knowledge of Egyptian history and politics. Inge Aflatun allowed me to work with her private collection of materials relating to women in Egyptian politics. Naula Darwish made her father's papers available to me.

Through Adil Amin and Mustafa Kamil Munib I was able to read the transcripts of political court cases in which communists were defendants. Joyce Blau gave me access to various records of the Egyptian communist movement. Muhammad al-Sayyid Ashmawi made introductions for me and provided me with publications relevant to my study.

From the historian Salah Isa I learned much about Egypt's past. This book profited from his political insights and his historical craftsmanship. Rifaat al-Said provided me a wide range of sources on the opposition movement and helped me formulate my ideas about leftist activity in Egypt. Shohrat al-Alim was a close and trusted friend and assisted me in a multitude of ways throughout my stay in Egypt.

Peter Gran encouraged this book from its inception and offered me his special knowledge of Egypt and international affairs. Zachary Lockman read this manuscript in a number of forms and offered important suggestions and criticisms. Sharif El Musa cheerfully helped me make sense out of some of the more obscure legal documents I had to examine and was always willing to discuss ideas. Judith Tucker, Beatrice Manz, and Irene Gendzier provided me with inspiration and friendship.

David Landes stimulated my interest in history and both through example and instruction demonstrated to me the rigors and rewards of serious academic scholarship. Albert Hourani was my first mentor in Middle Eastern Studies and has constantly been a guide and source of support. He read many versions of this book in dissertation and manuscript form, and his incisive criticisms contributed to the final product.

I am grateful to all the members of my family who gave me their confidence and helped me in countless ways. I especially want to thank Gertrude Botman, Agnes Birmingham, Nancy Birmingham, and Ethel

Green, who were always there when I needed them. Finally, my deepest gratitude is to my husband, Tom Birmingham, who shared in every stage of this work. He tolerated long absences while I was engaged in research. He patiently read many drafts of this manuscript and always offered meaningful suggestions. His comments improved the quality of this book immeasurably. In the end, of course, I take sole responsibility for the contents of this book.

I would also like to thank those at the American Research Center in Egypt and the Social Science Research Council for their financial support, and at the Middle East Center at Harvard University for allowing me to make use of the many resources of the university.

Introduction

EGYPTIAN SOCIETY during the twentieth century has undergone significant social, political, economic, and ideological transformations which have affected virtually every aspect of life for all the Egyptian people.

Before the 1952 coup d'etat, the overwhelming majority of Egyptians were *fallahin*, peasants, who lived along the narrow ribbon of the Nile River, where the soil was rich and the agricultural harvests abundant. For the vast majority of rural Egyptians living conditions were humble. Houses, for example, were simple mud-brick dwellings shared with farm animals and lacking even the most basic amenities. Diets were simple and deficient in essential food elements. The *fallahin* ate cereals, roots, cornbread, onions, and cheese, and only rarely fruit, milk, or meat. During the first half of the twentieth century industrial development progressed steadily, but Egypt remained essentially a rural country with agriculture contributing the largest share of the national income and providing employment for the great majority of the population.

The system of land ownership was highly unequal and geared to the benefit of the large landlords. Although they accounted for only a tiny percentage of the agricultural community, their disproportionate wealth brought the big landowners social standing in the countryside, political authority in Cairo, and economic power nationally. Landlords also commanded legislative power which allowed them to dictate policy and essentially to shape the development of the country.

The composition of the parliamentary cabinets is but one indication of this influence. Of the fifty cabinets formed in Egypt from that of Husayn Rushdi on April 5, 1914, to that of Ali Mahir on July 24,

1952, the landlords represented, on average, 58.35 percent of the membership. This was inclusive of Wafdist cabinets in which the majority of seats were also accounted for by agricultural interests. The cabinet of Mustafa al-Nahhas formed on February 4, 1942, for example, included 63.76 percent large landowners; his next cabinet, formed on May 26, 1942, contained 64.2 percent.[1]

Egyptian landlords were slow to invest in industry but those who did were usually supported by Bank Misr which was responsible for helping develop industrial and credit establishments. In the first half of the twentieth century, however, industry was controlled either by Europeans or by Egyptian minorities, mainly of foreign origin—*mutamassirun*—and although their role in the national economy was continually contracting during this time, they were always significant economically. Minority domination of the economic system affected not only the economy itself, but also the willingness of Egyptian agricultural interests to take risks and become industrial entrepreneurs.

Industrialists, merchants, professionals, bureaucrats, workers, craftsmen, and casual laborers were among those who lived in the towns and cities. In contrast to the upper classes, who lived very comfortably on tree-lined streets in architecturally interesting buildings, urban workers experienced overcrowded living conditions frequently coupled with ill health and malnutrition. A growing petty bourgeoisie consisting of government officials, teachers, tradesmen, and artisans also populated the urban space. This group was perhaps the most volatile politically, because its economic needs and social ambitions went largely unsatisfied in the conflict between low incomes and rising expectations. It was mainly from this stratum that the nonparliamentary communist and Islamic fundamentalist opposition stemmed.

World War I proved to be a watershed event in Egypt, and it unalterably changed the country for several important reasons. Conflict provided a potent stimulus to industrialization and self-sufficiency. New industries developed and fledgling operations were given a boost. War also offered the country fresh ideas, which led first to the establishment of a socialist and then a communist party. Alongside a small leftist opposition, a vibrant nationalist movement spread throughout the country. To all but a minority of people, the most compelling issue, by far, was the struggle for national independence from the British. National liberation became a rallying cry for Egyptians from all social classes, age groups, and places of residence. Fighting tenaciously and over time for sovereignty, Egyptians won their rights little by little, first in 1922 with limited independence, then in 1936 with the Anglo-Egyptian Treaty, then in 1952 as a result of the revolution, and finally in 1956 after the total evacuation of the British. The demand for local control over all the affairs of the country heightened political awareness and convinced important parts of the population of the immediate need for domestic reform.

In the early 1920s, Egypt adopted the European liberal tradition and styled its young and relatively open political system upon the experiences of western democracies. Led by a monarch whose disproportionate power and frequent interventions into politics often subverted the parliamentary system, the liberal experiment lasted from 1923 until Nasser's coup d'etat. It allowed for a multiplicity of political parties (albeit with restrictions), a wide range of newspapers, and a host of political clubs. This was a vital and dynamic period in Egypt's modern political history which has yet to be recreated. In the post-1952 period, Nasser forbade all independent political activity. After that, both Sadat and Mubarak, for different reasons, tempered true opposition and discouraged sustained criticism in fear of the instability that might arise.

During the middle years of the liberal age, in the latter 1920s and early 1930s, new concepts emerged and new organizations crystallized mirroring the nationalist mood in Egypt, the pains of the 1929 Depression, and the growth of fascism in Europe. The Muslim Brotherhood, Young Egypt, and antifascist groups which planted the seeds of the communist movement of the 1940s all came into their own and eventually left their marks on Egyptian society and politics. These organizations conceptualized the problems of Egyptian society and their solutions differently but were united in their rejection of Wafdist-style liberalism, which was seen as increasingly appeasing to the British and politically bankrupt.

The Muslim Brotherhood, founded by Hasan al-Banna, gained substantial support in the 1930s and 1940s from lower-middle-class and popularly based social groups. Its theocratic beliefs and calls for societal reform appealed to the more humble members of the Egyptian population. Ideologically, the organization was antiimperialist and advocated the ousting of the British from Egyptian soil. Its most active efforts were directed against secularism and liberalism, which were deemed contrary to Islamic values. Significantly, the Muslim Brotherhood became active in social and cultural affairs, education, and work-related issues: it set up schools, factories, and mosques in an attempt to fill the gap left by the state and to aid the lower classes.

The Brotherhood commanded its greatest influence after World War II, and although it was outlawed in 1954 by Abdul Nasser, it survived underground and left an important legacy in the Egyptian political arena.

Young Egypt was established in the 1920s in opposition to the existing system of parliamentary politics. It blended Pharaonic and chauvinistic attitudes with calls for social and economic reforms. Perhaps more than other groups in Egypt, it looked with favor on the fascist organizations of Europe and modeled itself in their image. The group went through several changes in form and ideology, and by the end of the 1940s, transformed itself into the Socialist Party of Egypt. By then, it concentrated on issues of economic interest, such as the inequality of land ownership and the gap between rich and poor, and it became associated with the Soviet Union in matters of foreign policy.

Egyptian antifascist organizations grew out of the European crisis of the 1930s. Totally opposed to the antisemitic, antidemocratic trends in the West, these groups supported the aims of the international peace movement and a return to relative harmony among diverse populations. The nascent left-wing movement of the 1940s in Egypt derived from these groups.

Egypt has gone through various stages of economic and political development in the post–World War II period. Those Egyptians who lived through the 1940s recall its militancy and its energy. This was a time of heightened nationalist momentum, Islamic fundamentalist organizing, and communist agitation, activity which flourished despite the conservatism of the king and his political entourage. It was a period of increasing political awareness for the majority of the country, of street demonstrations, labor unrest, and cumulative disenchantment. Such activity was in marked contrast to the era of Nasserism, which was politically uniform and less confrontational in consequence of the harsh police repression directed against anyone expressing oppositional views.

After 1952, the era of European-style liberalism was over. No one mourned its passing less than Gamal Abdul Nasser, who successfully engineered the overthrow of the royalist regime. During his tenure as president of Egypt, Nasser became active in Arab affairs and aimed at forging inter-Arab alliances under Egypt's leadership and protection. Nasser made Arab nationalism his personal message and emphasized the bond which he believed existed between all those who were Arab by language, history, and culture. For him, and many others of his generation, Arab nationalism was a bulwark against the manifold attacks of the rest of the world. People who remember Nasser often express mixed feelings: although many suffered from his rule, they can applaud policies which brought self-respect and a measure of independence to Egypt. His leadership in the Third World non-aligned movement, his anti-Americanism, his deep attachment to Arab nationalism, and his efforts to implement socialism still evoke powerful reactions, ranging from veneration to antipathy. His death in 1970 shocked and distressed almost the entire population, who unknowingly stood at the crossroads of a new phase of Egyptian history.

Only a short time later, the new president, Anwar Sadat, an undistinguished military officer who became a cunning and controversial world-class politician, engineered the "denasserization" of Egypt, which meant dramatic changes in the country's economic, political, and international stances. Determined to reclaim Egyptian land lost to Israel during the 1967 war, and unable to win diplomatic redress, Sadat elected to wage war against Israel in 1973. Egypt's highly respectable performance brought dignity back to the Arab armed forces and raised Sadat's stature at home. Making use of his new image as statesman and military hero, Sadat developed a close friendship with the United States. Later on, in 1977, he became the first Arab leader to visit Jerusalem. While there, he addressed the Israeli Knesset in an effort to ensure Israeli withdrawal from Arab land and to contain increasing unrest in Egypt. In addition, Egyptians were asked to support his vision of the future, his international alignment with the West, and his economic policies, which centered around *infitah*, a system designed to liberalize the economy and attract foreign investment. Sadat left a legacy following his assassination in 1981, but his passing did not evoke the massive grief and deeply felt sorrow manifested eleven years earlier when Nasser died.

For the third time in less than three decades, Egyptians looked on expectantly when a new president assumed office. This time they watched Hosni Mubarak make efforts to bring Egypt back into the Arab fold, to allow limited popular participation in the political process, and to clean up corruption. They hoped such action would lift Egypt out of its political and economic morass and begin a new era of progressive change.

Compared to his predecessors, Hosni Mubarak is much less of a charismatic figure. He is neither the captivating speaker that Nasser was, nor can he replicate Sadat's international stature. He does not, therefore, command the passionate emotions that his forerunners did. He is a quiet, mild-tempered man who has been on trial in the eyes of his population since taking office. He is respected as honest and efficient, but criticized for lacking the sophistication necessary to address the serious social and economic problems he inherited. Despite the best of intentions, Mubarak has yet to accomplish meaningful transformation: inflation remains high; the economy is very unstable; wages are dangerously low; the bureaucratic structure is so heavy that it retards development; and democratization has not yet been achieved.

While Egypt is largely an agricultural country, high population density and the accompanying pressures on infrastructural services characterize its urban life. In Cairo, for example, which houses a quarter of the country's population, services are woefully inadequate: the roads and sidewalks are badly broken, raw sewage festers openly in the street, traffic jams are ubiquitous, and housing is inadequate for the growing population.

Egypt is a very poor country which suffers from many of the problems endemic to the Third World. Yet, throughout the country people have been encouraged to develop high expectations. Television programs and commercials, magazine publicity, and billboard advertisements have contributed to increased public awareness of the possibility of a materially comfortable life. Inadvertently, the population has been set up for a massive let-down, for there is no realistic way the government can satisfy consumers' growing wants and hopes. Given the structure of Egyptian society, only a few people can improve their material existence substantially. Disappointment, therefore, could prove to be very dangerous for Mubarak—a president who lacks a natural constituency of his own to depend on.

Egypt is characterized by ethnic and religious homogeneity, since the overwhelming majority of Egyptians are Muslims. The Coptic Christian minority, which represents under 10 percent of the population, struggles to maintain its historic, religious, and cultural roots in a society undergoing a degree of Islamic resurgence. The uniformity of the population stands in contrast to the heterogeneity of the 1940s. At that time, too, the majority of Egyptians were Muslims with a substantial Coptic minority, but there were other thriving minority groups as well. The Greek, Italian, French, Armenian, and Jewish communities gave cities like Cairo and Alexandria an exciting cosmopolitan flavor. Members of ethnic and religious minorities played active, visible roles in Egyptian life, either as bankers, businessmen, and professionals, or as grocers, vendors, and skilled workers. They might have been resented for their wealth and status, but if they were not directly tied to the resident English population and the veiled occupation, they were, for the most part, accepted. The British, on the other hand, were openly and actively disliked by indigenous Egyptians for their unwillingness to leave the country and allow Egyptians total control.

The outbreak of the Palestine War in 1948 began a pivotal juncture in Egypt's modern history. As a direct result of the conflict, the ethnic heterogeneity of the country began to decrease. It was further reduced after the Suez War of 1956 and virtually extinguished after the nationalizations of 1961. As national self-awareness among Egyptians grew stronger, their traditional tolerance of ethnic minorities lessened. This form of patriotism was directed, especially, toward those non-Egyptians holding positions of authority. Although there are reminders in Egypt of the diversity characteristic of earlier decades—a few Greek grocers, Armenian jewelers, and French booksellers still carry on their trades—ethnically the country is quite uniform.

When Egyptians gained control of their country in 1952, for the first time since the Ottoman occupation of the early 1500s, an enormous symbolic and psychological victory was won. The population felt in control of all aspects of their existence. And from the fifties onward, real changes did occur: the businessmen, the money lenders, the department store owners, the bankers, the doctors, the decision makers, the technocrats, the military officers, and the administrative officials were of Egyptian, and not foreign or even ethnically European origin. At last, members of the indigenous culture were dominant.

Yet even with local control over Egyptian affairs, spiritual and material problems have caused the governments worry. At this time, Mubarak is being counseled to pay strict attention to his opposition, and in particular to the Islamic fundamentalist movement which has recently gained credibility and popularity among a substantial number of lower- and middle-class Egyptians. Because the religious groups pose a real threat to secular Egyptian institutions and leadership, they are taken more seriously by the authorities than are leftist dissidents. Disconnected and sporadic challenges to the administration have occurred, but Mubarak may be comforted, at present, by the fact that no real dialogue between the Islamic and secular opposition groups exists, and because fundamental philosophical and political differences separate the dissidents.

One notable exception to the diversity of the opposition is its common stand on international alignment. Both Marxists and fundamentalists believe that the United States is trying to take over where the Europeans left off at the end of the colonialist era. Since Egyptians have struggled so hard for their independence, they will not easily allow themselves to be controlled in their economic, political, intellectual, and social lives. To Egyptians of all political persuasions, national sovereignty is felt very deeply and will not be given up without a struggle. Mubarak must accommodate this deep and somewhat defensive form of Egyptian independence in devising his global policies.

Despite sustained efforts by all governments since Saad Zaghlul to eradicate Marxism in Egypt, communist influences have not been eliminated. The revolutionary left still exists as a small, outlawed movement whose significance is much more limited today than it was in the 1940s and early 1950s. Historically, Egyptian communism has been characterized by three striking features. First, the communist movement has rarely been unified. For most of the twentieth century it has been made up of separate and rival Marxist organizations. Diversity has led to fragmentation and interparty hostility which has weakened the impact of communism in the country. Second, there has been a noticeable dissociation between the communists and the Egyptian people. This is most obviously reflected in the composition of the movement, which has been middle class and was during the 1940s made up of ethnic minorities. Third, the communists have never created a mass movement or diffused their ideas beyond the narrow realm of intellectuals, some skilled workers, and a handful of peasants.

Although Marxists never succeeded in assuming power, they have contributed to the tradition of dissident thought which has become an important part of Egypt's political life. They have also exerted sporadic influence on nationalist, labor, and student affairs. Moreover, the political work carried out by the revolutionary left and the ideological positions it propagated helped create an atmosphere in which the Free Officers could operate. Partly because of leftist agitation in the 1940s, liberal nationalism did not exclusively dominate Egyptian politics in the post–World War II period. When the military accomplished their coup d'etat, they received widespread endorsement partly because of the earlier efforts of the left to undermine the ideological support for the royalist regime. Accordingly, when the Free Officers did act, their target was already largely discredited.

While the revolutionary left's dream of socialist revolution has never been realized, many of the radical policies adopted by the military leaders after the 1952 coup were communist-supported proposals. Land reform, alliance with socialist bloc countries, the policy of neutralism, and socialist economic planning were communist-developed ideas ultimately carried out by Nasser. Notwithstanding their limited participation in Nasser's government, the revolutionary left still believed that the policies it articulated shaped the direction of change in the country and contributed to domestic progress.

Despite structural inadequacies and limited recruitment, the communist movement of the past still exerts some influence on the political life of Egypt today. A significant part of the Egyptian left draws its inspiration and some of its leaders from the period of the 1940s, 1950s, and 1960s. This is shown in the Tagammu Party, a legal leftist opposition party which is an umbrella group of Nasserists, communists, liberals, and democrats. Created by the government in 1976, during Sadat's liberalization phase, it maintains an open presence and publishes a newspaper, an important activity in the Egyptian political tradition.

Even though its publication has a wide circulation and attracts a variety of readers, from members of the government to more humble Egyptians interested in political issues, the Tagammu Party (and the left generally) today faces serious problems. It has not yet learned how to find a language or a leadership which is able to reach the majority of Egyptians and convince them of the correctness of its views. A chronic problem for the left has been its failure to attract large numbers to party membership or to identify causes which can compel and sustain significant numbers of people. The left has not provided convincing answers to the domestic problems facing Egypt: most notably rapid population growth, adequate and affordable food and energy supplies, employment, personal income, incomplete democracy, and the role of women and minorities in society. Moreover, leftists have not yet convinced the population that their analysis of international politics is particularly incisive. The left's analysis of Egypt's alignment internationally, pan-Arabism, Palestinian national aspirations, and terrorism remain matters of generally esoteric interest to only a limited stratum of people. In addition, the left has not yet come to terms with vibrant organizations from which it has been historically alienated—in particular, the Islamic fundamentalist groups which have mass appeal, a radical vision, and active supporters.

Radicals active in the revolutionary left or the Tagammu Party are sometimes the very same people who led the communist movement of the 1940s and 1950s. Since the issues of organization and credibility which they struggled with decades ago have yet to be solved, the left's ability to influence political life in the country has yet to be maximized. Until it finds a way to become a mainstream force in Egypt, the left's hopes for changing the structure and character of the society will remain unfulfilled.

The following study represents an attempt to understand and explain the political traditions, organizations, and policies of the revolutionary left. Although the left failed to realize its most ambitious goals, its contributions to Egyptian intellectual life and its influence on Egyptian politics make the experience of communists worthy of study and consideration.

The Rise of Egyptian Communism, 1939–1970

1

The Roots of Egyptian Communism

Militant Politics in Post–World War I Egypt

By WORLD WAR I a strong nationalist movement directed against the British occupation had emerged in Egypt. After nearly forty years of dictatorship under British colonial administrators Cromer and Kitchener, the Egyptian population was no longer willing to tolerate English domination and called unequivocally for national independence. The patriotic and anti-British sentiment generated by Saad Zaghlul's deportation and inflamed by the 1919 Egyptian revolution was espoused by a broad section of the Egyptian population. Accompanying this nationalist fervor, the ideas of socialism and trade unionism were slowly gaining some prominence among very small circles of Egyptian and foreign-born intellectuals, and workers first of European and then Egyptian origin.

The nationalist and labor activity in the postwar period convinced radical intellectuals that the absence of a political party capable of leading or manipulating the unfolding class conflict was a serious problem. The situation called for the formation of a new and independent political force able to mobilize the disaffected members of Egyptian society. In response, the Egyptian Socialist Party (ESP) was organized in 1920 to take advantage of the dissident activity in the country.

The ESP, the genesis of the Egyptian left, was founded by a group of intellectuals who embraced the range of socialist ideas: Fabianism, social democracy, and Marxism. The party was created as a legal organization and designed as an umbrella group open to all shades of the Egyptian democratic opposition. Ideological diversity was also

1

linked to heterogeneity in the group's two sections. The Alexandrian branch was predominantly organized by and composed of the more marginal nationalities—Italians, Greeks, Armenians, and Jews. It attracted foreigners both at the leadership and rank-and-file levels, and was led by Joseph Rosenthal, a Jewish jeweler of Italian nationality and either Russian[1] or German extraction.[2] Because Alexandria was the center of trade union agitation at the time and the hub of nascent socialism, it was a highly suitable place for a socialist party to develop. In contrast, the Cairo branch recruited mostly Egyptians, and Salama Musa and Mahmud Husni al-Arabi were among its members. Salama Musa was the first propagator of socialism in Egypt and an important intellectual who wrote many books and articles on social justice, reform, and education. Ideally, he looked forward to the establishment of a socialist "society," a group whose aim would be to study domestic and world conditions rather than to act upon them. Despite the significance of having recruited Musa, soon after this group was established it became internally divided and lost both its membership and its dynamism to the Alexandrian organization.

In the first two years of its life, the ESP focused on a narrowly defined British colonialism as Egypt's sole problem; even colonialism's local agents in business and agriculture were ignored. The failure even to attempt to confront the problem of indigenous collaboration with foreign domination suggests the superficiality of the party's theoretical stance and the immaturity of the organization itself. Moreover, although imperialism received major attention in the party's programs, the members planned little real activity against the British forces in Egypt. Paradoxically, on those occasions when the ESP did make real interventions they were directed against Egyptian nationals in agriculture and industry. As a result, a strange schizophrenia characterized the party: its theoretical positions ignored Egyptian collaboration with the British, while its political activity was directed almost exclusively against Egyptian capitalists.

As a consequence, the party prompted the hostility of the Wafd Party—the premier nationalist party in Egypt. Led by Saad Zaghlul, a hero celebrated by most of the population for his uncompromising attitude toward the British occupation of Egypt, the Wafd was seen at this time by an increasing number of Egyptians as representing the unity of the entire country. Hence, the Socialist Party was criticized as recklessly dividing the unanimity of the nation and irresponsibly challenging the nationalist leadership of Saad Zaghlul at a time when cooperation was needed to confront the British. The years 1919 and

1920, after all, were among the most dynamic in Egypt's nationalist history, when virtually the whole population supported the movement for national liberation. Yet, the left never fully grasped the depth of the nationalist opposition and could never become the heirs of the 1919 revolution. Instead of capitalizing on the revolt, harnessing nationalist fervor, and organizing the rage of the workers and peasants who had been supplied with arms and had fought against the British occupation, the primary efforts of the left were concentrated on waging limited labor strikes in factories, especially among ethnic workers.

In 1922, the party entered its second stage of development, when it was recast as the country's first communist party. With this radicalization, the factionalism which already existed in the party became intensified. Salama Musa and the more pacific intellectuals were being left behind by the aggressive direction in which the group was moving. They withdrew from the group in protest, unable to agree to the resolutions being adopted at the party's first conference. The radical leadership decided to transfer the party's administrative center from Cairo to Alexandria, unqualifiedly embrace communism, and elect a new central committee.

The new Egyptian Communist Party (ECP) joined the Comintern and, in the tradition of its socialist predecessor, continued to concentrate its efforts on the labor movement. It considered the development of trade unions and the leadership of the class struggle as its most important challenges. By 1923 it could in fact claim influence over a confederation of twenty or more labor organizations, many of which engaged in militant strike action.[3] Exercising an important effect on gas workers, electrical workers, tram workers, diverse textile workers, workers in the public utility companies, and workers of the Suez Petroleum refineries, the members of the ECP were quite effective in organizing Egyptian labor. In essence, they assumed they could play the most productive role in the political life of the country through their contacts with and influence over the organized proletariat.

The strength of the party amongst workers did not go unobserved by the youthful Wafdist government. Neither was the ECP unmindful of the rise of the Wafd as the prominent nationalist party in Egypt. Wishing to test the new government in 1924, the communists challenged Zaghlul's authority by directing workers in Alexandria to strike in demand of the recognition of trade unions and an eight-hour workday.[4] By urging this action, the ECP was demanding of Zaghlul a radical change in the government's attitude toward workers. When Zaghlul did not cede to the demands, the workers struck and took over the Egyptian Oil Company (Egoil) and the Alexandria textile factories (Filatures Nationales). A showdown between Zaghlul's government and the Communist Party was imminent.

To be sure, Zaghlul could not allow the communists to exert their influence over workers in open defiance of the government at this early stage of Egyptian independence. Although the left was not a major force in Egyptian society, its activities proved menacing to the newly constituted government and as a result Saad Zaghlul was compelled to squash the movement. He acted decisively by sending a battalion of infantrymen to Alexandria to end the labor disturbances and arrest the ringleaders. Later in the year, the entire party leadership was interned for spreading revolutionary doctrines and advocating the change of the social system by violent means. The communist-oriented Confederation of Trade Unions was disbanded, and in its place was formed a nationalist labor organization, the General Union of Workers, under the leadership of Wafdist lawyers Muhammad Thabit and Zuhayr Sabri.[5] Thus did Zaghlul cripple the left-leaning workers' movement.

Deprived of its leadership, and with its relationship with trade unions undermined, the ECP was severely weakened. Although individual members tried to revive the party, either alone or with help from the Comintern during the next decade, their efforts went unrewarded. Communism became an illegal, isolated, and marginal political current so that by 1935 the Party was no longer identified as a member of the Third International, and in 1943 its name did not appear as a signatory for the dissolution of the Comintern.

The ECP suffered a number of serious deficiencies. Although in its early years it could organize sections of the labor force in skilled industries, it never recruited workers in significant numbers because its message was simply not compelling at the time. In the early 1920s, workers were separated by skill, ethnic origin, language, and belief. Organized laborers of a leftist bent were mostly of foreign descent, and their political sentiments did not reflect the views of the majority of the Egyptian population. As a result of its almost exclusive ties to minority workers, the party was identified as alien and distrusted. For its entire life it remained outside the truly vital nationalist movement and divorced from the mainstream of political life in the country.

Had the left concentrated its energies on the national liberation struggle, or at least coordinated its efforts on the labor and nationalist fronts, it might have gained some credibility and been respected as a national force. Perhaps it could have attracted a larger, more Egyptian, and more socially diverse membership. Its intensive focus on the narrow class issue, however, exposed a serious miscalculation regarding the motivations behind Egyptian political activity at the time. By misjudging the general political sentiment and concentrating exclusively on working-class issues, the leadership condemned the party to a marginal existence.

Between the mid-1920s and the mid-1930s, there was a vacuum in the Egyptian Marxist movement reflecting the general stagnancy of radical political activity. After the reinstitution of the Constitution in 1935, however, political life in general became less uniform. The country began hearing the bolder oppositional voices of the Wafd, the Muslim Brotherhood, and Young Egypt, and witnessed the rise of their paramilitary organizations. Antifascist sentiment was also expressed by liberals and democrats. Among this group were Jewish Egyptians, especially, who established contacts with self-identified foreign Marxists living in the country. Marxists from the Armenian, Italian, and Greek communities were tied to the communist parties in their own countries and were not directly active in the Egyptian political field. These minorities did, however, maintain links with Egyptian Jewish intellectuals which were significant because they lent experience to the cause of antifascism, and because they contributed to the revival of indigenous Marxist thinking in the country through their diffusion of radical ideas. Egyptian Marxism of the late 1930s and early 1940s became associated with Jews through the antifascist movement.

Radicalized members of the Jewish minority set up clubs or "circles" of political, cultural, and intellectual activity. Egyptian Muslims and Copts participated, but to a much lesser extent. These clubs served as important centers for meeting like-minded people, for exchanging ideas, and learning more about the world in which these young adults lived. Such informal activity enhanced intellectual and social development and stimulated the minds of youth who were, for reasons of education and experience, favorably predisposed to internationalism and the left. Jewish Marxists who were particularly involved in legal antifascist and democratic activity in the 1930s acted, in the early 1940s, to create the clandestine communist movement which forms the subject of this work.

The Renewal of Radical and Antifascist Political Activity

Despite the demise of organized Egyptian communism in 1924, small pockets of legal leftist activity appeared in the cosmopolitan community of Egyptianized Europeans some years later. In the late 1920s or early 1930s, for example, Leon Castro, a wealthy Jewish lawyer and journalist, founded Les Essayistes, a scientific-cultural society which attracted a membership of Jewish, Italian, Greek, Syrian, and a small number of Egyptian intellectuals.[6] Castro himself was a leftist Zionist, and he was active in trying to mobilize minority Egyptian intellectuals against anti-Semitism. He encouraged campaigns against Nazism and called for the boycott of German goods and literature.

Diverse trends coexisted in the group: there were liberals, democrats, left-Zionists, and secular leftists. The purpose of the group was to allow intellectuals to study and comment on ideas of general interest and concern. The tolerance and openness which characterized the group allowed alternative views to develop which paved the way for members to break from the parent organization and form new units more suited to the individuals' particular political and ideological orientations.

Later, in 1934, Paul Jacot Descombes founded the Union of Peace Supporters. Some of its members were drawn from Les Essayistes. Descombes, of Swiss Protestant origin, was born in Cairo, where his father, an engineer, owned a contracting company. He was educated in Egypt's foreign schools and at the beginning of 1930, he traveled to Germany to pursue higher studies in music. There he was exposed to socialist and democratic ideas and established ties to the German Communist Party, though he was not a member. When he was home in Egypt on school vacation in 1933, Hitler came to power in Germany, and Descombes decided to remain in Egypt. He then began his short but noteworthy career as an Egyptian politician and ideologue.

Descombes's experience in Germany convinced him of the necessity to begin political activity in Egypt. He wanted to contact Egyptian workers and encourage political militancy using the classic model of Marxist organization, but he recognized the prematurity of such a gesture. Instead, the first step he took was to contact and initiate discussions with the people he knew most closely; it was natural that they consisted of Europeanized Egyptians and especially Greeks and Italians. Although he began working with the Greek communists and principally with Sakellaris Yannakakis, their leader, he soon became dissatisfied with the self-imposed isolation of the group. Since their activities were confined almost exclusively to fellow Greeks and their focus really lay outside Egypt itself, their influence on Egyptian affairs could hardly be more than negligible.

Descombes was convinced that a more indigenous Egyptian route to mobilization was necessary. He decided that the most expedient means of engaging Egyptians and becoming involved in Egyptian society was to establish a legal platform which formally displayed a democratic, antifascist, and antiwar character, yet actually operated as a front group for leftist activity. In that way, the government and occupation authorities were unlikely to interfere. To this end, the Union of Peace Supporters was organized and established connections with the international parent organization, Rassemblement Universel pour la Paix.

The Egyptian peace group was composed largely of people in their late teens or in early adulthood. They were college students, essentially of European origin and culture, who felt the immediacy of the antifascist campaign and welcomed the founding of the group. The secondary students recruited into the Union of Peace Supporters were also minority Egyptians who were educated in Cairene or Alexandrian *lycées* and were exposed to leftist ideas by their teachers, who openly popularized radical causes.[7] These students were brought up with an interest in international affairs and were acutely aware of the struggle against Nazism. Accordingly, they constituted an audience sympathetic to leftist ideas.

Raymond Aghion was one such youth. From a rich Alexandrian Jewish family, he gravitated to the left in the 1930s and joined the Union of Peace Supporters. He assessed his left-wing opinions in a personal way, but his feelings can be applied more generally to others in the cosmopolitan community.

> We were a small group of foreigners who all knew one another and talked with one another. For me, we lived in Egypt as foreigners. I frequently visited Europe and was dazzled by it. When I returned to Egypt I would feel that things were not moving in the right direction. I formed, in the beginning, utopian socialist ideas. I read Rousseau, Victor Hugo, then I would go down from the house into the street and feel what Victor Hugo described of the misery present in Egypt. . . . There was another problem: the victory of Hitler and the fear of the Jews. I, being a Jew, felt what many Jews were feeling—the necessity of relying on the democratic movement against fascism. I slowly came closer to the leftist movement.[8]

Publicly, the Union of Peace Supporters sponsored lectures which were cultural and political in substance; they focused on art, literature, the civil war in Spain, the nationalist war in China, and the Italian attack in Ethiopia. The Union educated its members about the current political issues of the day and asked sympathizers to contribute money to causes such as that of the Spanish Republicans.[9]

With the outbreak of World War II, the members of the Union of Peace Supporters believed that their organization no longer had a *raison d'etre,* and it was dissolved from within. At the same time, many of its members formed another organization, Le Groupe Études, whose purpose was to encourage study of Egyptian society.[10] Among the studies prepared by members of Le Groupe Études was the book *Egypt Now,* published in English and directed mainly to the Allied soldiers stationed in Egypt.[11] Its intent was to provide foreign troops with historical and contemporary information about the country. It included translations of poems and short stories, as well as a guide for getting to know Egypt. It was a well-written handbook and undoubtedly instructive to those who read it. Ironically, a moving poem, "The Egyptian Worker," by the poet Bairam al-Tunsi, appeared in translation. Its message, however, suggests the group's radicalization and inclination toward issues of popular social justice.

> I sew shoes for you, and walk in the dirt;
> I plump up mattresses for you,
> > and live squatting in a shack.
> > Is this my due, my portion?
> > Let God settle the accounts!
> You live in proud houses, but it is I who build them;
> You sleep in silken sheets,
> > but it's I who wove them;
> You own rivers of gold,
> > but it's I who made them flow.
> > With God there is no envy;
> > But I, I score it up against you.
> From dawn to dusk the hammer is in my hands,
> Workday and holiday alike I bear it.
> The sun of the streets is warm,
> > While I shiver in my rags,
> > And watch you flinch as I pass by—
> > Too low to be spoken to.
> I house you, clothe you, feed you
> > and then you treat me so!

> On the day of my death there will be
>   no money for a coffin.
> And you, for my last journey,
>   Will grudge me even a sigh.[12]

Despite the indigenous perspective expressed in "The Egyptian Worker," Le Groupe Études remained confined to a predominantly non-native membership. While most participants supported the group's nonconfrontational aim—the better understanding of Egyptian society —there existed a small minority of more militant members. Ahmad Sadiq Saad, Yusuf Darwish, and Raymond Duwayk, three Egyptian Jews whom we will encounter later on as well, fell into this latter category. More politicized than many of their colleagues, they were determined to work within the Egyptian community, and since they spoke Arabic well, unlike a great number of the cosmopolitan community, they had access to Egyptian society.

Paul Jacot Descombes befriended the three young men. He got to know and trust them, and among all his comrades, he saw them as the best possible organizers of a truly Egyptian communist party. Descombes recognized the need for establishing a party and recruiting Egyptians into it, but he believed this was a task Egyptians themselves had to undertake; he considered Sadiq Saad, Raymond Duwayk, and Yusuf Darwish so qualified by virtue of their Egyptian (albeit Jewish) birth. In contrast, Descombes always felt himself an outsider in Egypt, a temporary Swiss visitor.

It is the contention of Rifaat al-Said, who has written widely on Egyptian communism, that no communist party was established in the prewar period because Descombes shirked responsibility and refused to organize his left-wing colleagues.[13] Unlike others in the left movement, according to al-Said, Descombes's experience and wide contacts would have best suited him to the role of party organizer and, perhaps, even leader. The validity of this proposition is, however, open to question. Paul Jacot Descombes was, to be sure, a novice in political life and a beginner in both the study and practice of Marxism. He was, for the most part, ensconced within the foreign community. He may have had grand hopes for the Egyptian left, but in reality he possessed few plans to fulfill them. Separated from the hub of Egyptian society, he was isolated from the very people whose conditions he believed needed improvement.

Those who were associated with Descombes were themselves newcomers to the worlds of politics and theory. They may have felt passionately for the plight of the poor and the dispossessed, but at that time they were young idealists with very few contacts with the popular classes.

Against al-Said's charge, it must be said that Descombes's belief that an outsider should not organize the communist movement seems eminently sensible, given the colonial history of Egypt. Egypt was a semi-occupied country, and its population carried with it the legacy of foreign domination. Foreigners and semiforeigners almost always had better jobs, higher salaries, more elegant apartments, and better lifestyles than their Egyptian counterparts. This contrast, constantly observed by the native Egyptians, naturally created feelings of animosity. The often-felt prejudices and the arrogance of foreigners, plus their cavalier treatment of Egyptians, compounded the separation between the disparate cultures.

Moreover, within the prevailing Egyptian political framework, neither foreigners nor Egyptianized Europeans as a group ever established a real place for themselves. Except for a handful of ethnic politicians, those of foreign origin simply did not participate in politics; instead, they engaged in other forms of public activity, such as business or the liberal professions.

When Ahmad Sadiq Saad, Yusuf Darwish, and Raymond Duwayk founded the ethnically mixed Youth Group for Popular Culture in the early 1940s, this was considered unconventional, at best. The immediate goal of the youth group was to improve the educational level of the popular classes and by doing so to advance literacy. In addition to training in the Arabic language, there were classes in mathematics, history, and civil rights. Two centers were set up: one in Bulaq for workers and one in the Cairo suburb Mit Aqba for peasants. Hilmi Yassin, a native Egyptian active in politics in the 1940s and 1950s, recalled one of his own experiences in the Mit Aqba group:

> I went to the mosque and after the Friday prayer I spoke with the peasants. I told them, "We are a group of youth from Cairo who had the good opportunity to study and learn. Now we are ready to teach you the things you missed and we have opened a center to educate you. There is no charge." All that we needed was the rent of the room — fifty piasters; that meant that the peasants paid one or two piasters. I handed out the timetable of the lessons. People were happy to know that we came to teach them and they started to participate.[14]

Caution was the hallmark of Sadiq Saad, Yusuf Darwish, and Raymond Duwayk; they were careful not to hasten, prematurely, the political activity of their associates. For instance, during the first years that Hilmi Yassin worked with them, between 1939 and 1945, he never heard uttered the words "Marxism" or "communism." As a result, he saw the youth group as simply a public-service, community-oriented project which trained sympathetic Egyptian youth to help workers and peasants acquire a rudimentary education. Yassin considered his "mentors" nationalists and community organizers. Only years later, when his commitment to change had been firmly established, was he brought into their confidence and into their inner world of underground communist activity.

In 1942, the Italian and German forces entered the borders of the Western Desert of Egypt. Jews in Egypt began assessing their situation and some, fearful of an Axis victory and the subsequent Nazi control of Egypt, migrated to Palestine.[15] Sadiq Saad, Raymond Duwayk, and Yusuf Darwish discussed their positions as Jews and as Egyptians and decided that it would be an error to leave the country. On the contrary, they believed it was necessary to stay in Egypt and fight the fascist forces. Their decision to remain cemented their alliance and strengthened their determination to pursue shared political goals. After al-Alamayn, they separated from Descombes and began working on their own.

Yusuf Darwish was a lawyer who represented several small trade unions in legal cases. Through his work, he was able to make a connection with some of the labor leaders in the textile mechanics union in Shubra al-Khayma. In particular, he met Mahmud al-Askari, Taha Saad Uthman, and Muhammad Yusuf al-Mudarrik who, one after another, took part in the Youth Group for Popular Culture and continued for a long time as cornerstones of the labor movement. Together they were instrumental in establishing the Workers' Committee for National Liberation in 1945, which aspired to become the political body of the working class, and published the workers' newspaper *al-Damir*. While Darwish involved himself in union affairs, Raymond Duwayk and Sadiq Saad worked in Egyptian intellectual circles. They participated in the Committee for Spreading Modern Culture, a cultural society for many rising Egyptian intellectuals, and with Ahmad Rushdi Salih they founded the magazine *al-Fajr al-Jadid*, the New Dawn. Committed to radicalizing journalism in Egypt, they also inaugurated the Twentieth Century Publishing House. These cultural activities displaced the role of the Youth Group for Popular Culture, which was dissolved.

Ahmad Sadiq Saad, Raymond Duwayk, and Yusuf Darwish were not alone in the cultural and political fields. (See Figure 1.) In the late 1930s, the Democratic Union was also set up, with the Egyptianization of the leftist movement as its theme. The Union perceived itself as being the first Marxist-oriented political group constituted after the dissolution of the Egyptian Communist Party. Marcel Israel, Henri Curiel, and Hillel Schwartz, three of the future leaders of the Egyptian Marxist movement, emerged as prominent figures in this organization. Before long, though, personal, tactical, and ideological differences among the three led to the break-up and disappearance of the Union. Significantly, the clashes that occurred caused political divisions to freeze into a pattern which haunted the Egyptian communist movement for the whole decade of the 1940s and in fact far beyond.

The "Trotskyite" Tendency

Although there were moments during the 1940s when it was possible to locate a self-identified "Trotskyite" tendency within the sphere of oppositional politics, Trotskyism for the most part was an insignificant movement, confined to a small intellectual circle of young Egyptians. While there were limited and sporadic efforts to reach a broader base of the Egyptian population, this brand of Marxist thought never gripped even a small segment of the popular classes. Instead, it was an ideology of a tiny minority within the Marxist movement as a whole. It deserves comment, however, because as an oppositional current it was attractive principally to indigenous Egyptians who, in contrast with more orthodox Marxists, carried Egyptian nationality.

Trotskyism was never formally defined by its followers in Egypt. Rather, in Trotsky's ideas some activist intellectuals found a convenient vehicle to detach themselves from the largely cosmopolitan composition of Egypt's radical left. Trotskyites were, in the main, highbrow intellectuals who prided themselves on their authenticity as Egyptians.

Art et Liberté, the first avowedly Trotskyite group, was a legal entity founded at the end of 1939 by a group of Egyptian artists and literary figures, among whom were Georges Henein, Ramsis Yunan,

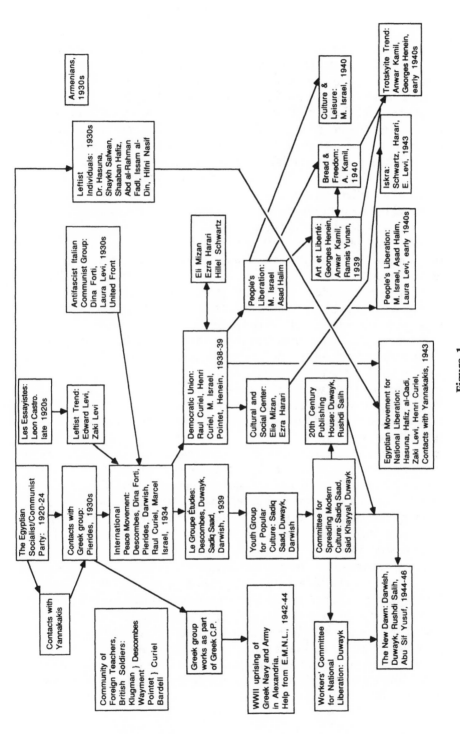

Figure 1
A Map of the Leftist Movement

Anwar Kamil, Lutfallah Sulayman, and Kamil al-Tilmisani. The goals of the group were to arrange for the publication of avant-garde cultural works, to acquaint Egyptian youth with the arts movement in Europe, and to advance literature and the arts in Egypt.[16] The group began by publishing a bulletin, al-Tatawwur (Evolution) the first number entirely in French and the second in both French and Arabic. It is an ironic twist that while the members were almost exclusively indigenous Egyptians, the language of discourse primarily used was French—the language of aristocratic and cosmopolitan Egypt. As a result, the audience capable of appreciating the form and being influenced by the content of the group's ideas was extremely limited.

Art et Liberté also organized art exhibitions in Cairo, the first of which took place at the Sulayman Pasha Club in January 1940, after the publication of the first issues of al-Tatawwur. Other exhibitions were arranged—in Cairo in 1941 at the Imobilia Building, in 1942 at the Continental Hotel, in 1944 and 1945 at the lycée français. The members viewed this as a major effort toward the exposure of surrealist art in Egypt. Surrealism was the badge of the artists associated with the group, and painters Fuad Kamil (who was the brother Anwar, one of the association's organizers), Ramsis Yunan, and Kamil al-Tilmisani tried to break down the conventional views of aesthetic appreciation by presenting their works at these events.

Al-Tatawwur was the group's most successful operation. As the first socialist magazine in Egypt, al-Tatawwur was a highly sophisticated and well-regarded journal. Between January and September 1940, seven issues were circulated: five in magazine form and the last two as newspapers. It was read predominantly by cultured intellectuals who were interested by the avant-garde and socially conscious orientation of the articles. The journal addressed such issues as women's rights,[17] education,[18] the role of the United States in international affairs,[19] and social reform.[20] There were numerous articles on philosophy, art, and literature—with Arabic translations of Albert Cossery's short stories of popular Egypt.

Though a significant journal, al-Tatawwur could not sustain comparable political activity. The group existed as a conventional organization with a formal meeting place only from 1939 until 1941; after that the group became less structured. People assembled together periodically in private houses mainly to discuss cultural issues. As a cohesive group the circle languished and was, in fact, being superceded by a sister organization, Pain et Liberté, which was emerging in June 1940.

Art et Liberté and Pain et Liberté were very different organizations, as their names suggest. While the first concentrated almost exclusively on culture and literature, the second moved in a more materialist direction, one that had at least the potential of attracting a wider membership. Whereas the art group appealed only to middle- and upper-class Egyptians, Pain et Liberté tried to draw a more humble membership of lower- and middle-class recruits, and it had some limited successes among individual textile and aviation workers.[21]

Pain et Liberté used nearly the same organizational forms as did Art et Liberté, but an important difference lay in content and accent. When Pain et Liberté organized lectures, for example, the focus was on Egypt's social, economic, and political problems: poverty, ignorance, and the class system that perpetuated them; the need for reforming the political parties; the economic relationships between workers and capitalists, and between peasants and landlords; democracy and the popular government.[22]

In the early 1940s, Pain et Liberté attracted the attention of police authorities and was branded as a subversive group made up of indigenous Egyptians. Perhaps because of its Egyptian composition, sixteen members of Pain et Liberté were arrested for subversive activity in 1942 and interned for one year. The arrests demonstrated to the opposition as a whole that the police forces were knowledgeable about the legal dissident movement and, moreover, capable of moving against it. The group was badly hurt by the police action, both numerically and operationally: while it lived on until 1946, it did so in a very truncated and quiescent form.

In reality, Trotskyism as a political and ideological movement was barely visible in Egyptian society. Although the leaders identified themselves as Trotskyite sympathizers and considered themselves a separate and homogeneous Egyptian group, with no foreigners in the top ranks of the organization and no equals amongst the intellectuals of the left, the group accomplished very little.[23] The label of "Trotskyism," it seems, was little more than a convenient device used to distinguish the organization from mainstream leftist thought and action in Egypt and to separate it from the cosmopolitan elite, whose methods of direct action and whose support for pro-Soviet platforms were unacceptable.

In the end, the group simply withered away. Lacking a solid and committed leadership, it never generated meaningful and lasting activity. Because it was unable to withstand the pressure of the authorities and the consequent arrests and periods of imprisonment, it did not develop popular political roots. In addition, rival groups absorbed members of Pain et Liberté into their own more vital organizations, especially during the internment periods. And finally, perhaps the major cause of collapse was the group's organizational inexperience and theoretical ambiguity. Behind its lofty slogans, the organization was a hollow shell which never developed a concrete program and never captured the spirit of more than a handful of people. In essence, it existed as a clique of independent, isolated socialists, estranged from the communist movement in Egypt and incapable of contributing in any significant way to either the nationalist movement or leftist politics.

2

A Portrait of the Communist Movement

Communist Activists

THE ACTIVISTS who founded and participated both in the legal study groups and the antifascist circles of the 1930s emerged in the 1940s as dissidents eager to establish concrete political groups which reflected their developing social and political consciousness. The British occupation, Egypt's grinding poverty, and the material and cultural deprivation suffered by the mass of the population led numbers of young people in the early 1940s to embrace a doctrine which, at least theoretically, endorsed better conditions for all. The unremitting degree of control, manipulation, and restriction exercised by the mainstream political parties in Egypt further impelled militants to oppose the prevailing system which had proven incapable of finding solutions to the problems paralyzing the country. If the perceived hollowness of the democratic process enraged the leftists, then Egyptian subservience to the British provoked them into action. Proudly nationalist, though alienated from traditional political society, the communists hoped to transform Egypt's national culture, political structure, and economic affairs.

The communists stood outside conventional political life, which from the post–World War I period took the form of a struggle between the British, the Palace, the Wafd, and the minority parties. Political status was determined by family prominence, wealth, connections, and patronage. Landowners, capitalists, and representatives of the liberal professions controlled the political arena. Personal rivalries among the Egyptian political leadership were rife, and instability was inherent in the political process. The parliamentary system in place

17

since 1923 never really worked efficiently. As a result of intraparty clashes, closed political cliques, rigged elections, voting fraud, and repeated abrogations of the Constitution, a sound and vigorous system of government was impossible. Liberalism, in the Western sense, was operating at best only imperfectly, and the extreme left found no place within its domain.

The men and women who became communists in the early 1940s did so without the benefit of an established Marxist political tradition in Egypt. Because of the very brief experience of the first Communist Party in the early 1920s, and the virtual absence of communist activity through the decade of the 1930s, those who became communists during the Second World War were not "born into" the role. The militants of the 1940s were, on the contrary, themselves beginners and creators.

The Egyptian communist movement from World War II was made up of diverse organizations and was characterized by factionalism and dissension: there was no single, unified party. This was seemingly unimportant to the young Marxists who, organized in underground groups, were self-sacrificing in the extreme. Involvement in illegal activity meant that every aspect of their lives was affected: family ties, work, friendships, personal aspirations. A commitment to the party implied promises of time, discipline, obedience, and hard work. Moreover, terms in prison were an ever present threat, and most Egyptian communists served their share of sentences as political prisoners.

In post–World War II Egypt, being sympathetic to the disadvantaged did not necessarily imply being a communist. However, what distinguished the revolutionary left from reformist intellectuals was its hope for a complete restructuring of Egyptian society. Neither prison sentences, police hounding, job dislocation, nor confrontations with competing activists weakened the communists' resolve, mainly because of their faith in the integrity and correctness of their views.

The Composition of the Communist Movement

A profile of the communist movement will provide useful empirical information about the kinds of people recruited into leftist circles. While the sources do not allow for detailed statistical and demographic analyses, it is possible to gain insight into the world of communist culture through a discussion of the general composition of the membership. To that end, the following comments will highlight the involvement of students, intellectuals, workers, women, and Jews in the communist underground. Examining a member's place of origin, age, ethnic background, social class, and gender will allow for a concrete and somewhat personalized view of the movement. This information has the merit of demystifying the population of radicals and removing them from the world of secrecy and seclusion. Now familiar, the leftists themselves become easier to understand and their activity more comprehensible.

Communists had roots in Upper Egypt and the Delta, in Cairo and Alexandria. Although they originally came from towns, villages, and the larger cities, their involvement in underground activity dated, for the most part, from their arrival in Cairo or Alexandria to work or study. The communist movement was profoundly urban, and those who became involved did so after being exposed to its ideas in the factory or in the academy. Not surprisingly, Cairo became the center of communist activity and the home of the overwhelming majority of the membership. Those who migrated to the capital and those who were born there, with few exceptions, stayed once they arrived. It was, of course, the location of the nation's largest university and the focus of Egypt's political and economic life. The movement did extend beyond Cairo, but its heart never left there.

While diverse social backgrounds were represented in the movement, in the main the communists were of bourgeois and petty-bourgeois origin. There were the sons and daughters of landlords, there were even the children of a few distinguished pashas, and there were those with working class roots; but from 1939 to 1970, leftists were inescapably middle class. Most middle-class communists were attracted to the movement when they were under twenty-five years old. They were introduced to the ideas of Marxism and to the political situation of an occupied and dependent Egypt when they were primarily of high school and university age. Student interest in the political arena was not surprising since, from the 1919 revolution, students in Egypt were among the most politicized sectors of the society. Assembled in an intellectual environment, they had the leisure to think about the issues of the day and were naturally concerned about the future. Student life made them extremely sensitive to political and social events, permitted the study of other countries and traditions, and encouraged freedom of thought and imagination—all of which allowed them to entertain new ideas and challenge existing ones. The educated younger generation formed a political avant-garde whose intellectual and ideological curiosity was always widening.[1]

The student movement, which was nationalist, anti-British, and highly vocal, occupied a significant place in Egypt's political life from the early days of the twentieth century. Until World War II, the movement was basically Wafdist in orientation; after the end of hostilities, dissident political tendencies began to mature.[2] Marxist groups, members of the left-leaning Wafdist Vanguard, and independent democrats organized in the academy, collaborated in the national movement and notably influenced its direction. In the process, the leftist coalition made efforts to isolate and weaken the Muslim Brotherhood and Young Egypt which were the main opponents to the progressive alliance in the university. For the great majority of those attracted to the left, affiliation with Young Egypt or the Muslim Brotherhood was inconceivable. The Muslim Brotherhood was an essentially conservative religious organization which rejected political parties, condemned the West, and was suspicious of non-Muslim groups, especially those of Egyptian origin. Its members championed a literal interpretation of the Quran, the return to pure Islam, the necessity of *jihad*, and the segregation of women from men. These ideas and lifestyles were inherently incompatible with the cosmopolitan ethnic minorities who, in the main, made up the early membership of the communist movement.

Young Egypt was a paramilitary organization which in the mid and latter 1930s demonstrated admiration for the accomplishments of fascist regimes in Europe. In the eyes of the leftists, Young Egypt was totally discredited. Young Jews, Italians, and Greeks, in particular, who established relations with the Marxist movement were alienated by Ahmad Husayn's visit to Germany in 1938 and were hostile to his approval of fascism. Moreover, the organization's highly nationalist and antiforeign bent, symbolized in the slogan "God, Fatherland, and the King," was unacceptable to leftists whose national roots or cultural world derived from Europe and whose inclinations were internationalist.

Because the communists were secular, internationalist and, above all, cosmopolitan, they could find no place for themselves politically in either Young Egypt or the Muslim Brotherhood. Neither could emerging leftists accommodate themselves intellectually to the tenets of fascism or fundamentalism. Despite the fact that the left, Young Egypt, and the Muslim Brotherhood all identified many of the same problems, their solutions and their visions of Egypt's future were so fundamentally incompatible that sustained mutual affiliations were never possible at the time.

The radicalism of the student movement was chronicled in the short-lived newspaper, *al-Talia* (The Vanguard). Published between September 1945 and June 1946, left-wing ideas predominated; articles about socialism and imperialism appeared regularly and reports about strikes and demonstrations were commonplace. As noted in the newspaper, in the immediate postwar period, the student movement mirrored the mood of the nation. It was restless, detached from the political mainstream and in search of a new direction. It resented the King, smarted at the unfulfilled promises made by the British during the war, and was offended by the presence of occupation forces. Closely allied with the radical student population were leftist professionals and intellectuals, and in particular, teachers, lawyers, doctors, artists, poets, novelists, and journalists who sympathized with the aims and intentions of the defiant youth movement. Because educated leftists in and out of the academy often traveled in common circles, they knew one another fairly intimately and could easily collaborate in political activity. Being of roughly similar age, they were united by similar generational experiences and comparable views of political life in Egypt.

Actually, the circumstances that produced the radical student movement also gave rise to an independent and politically active workers' movement which also helped diffuse Marxist ideas in the country. The workers who were influenced by the left, though smaller in numbers, were only slightly older than the students and intellectuals when they embraced revolutionary ideas. They were moved by the communists' explanations of class relations and by the political and economic goals of the left. Labor's new leadership, which included socialists, communists, and independent radicals, played an important part in raising class consciousness among rank and file workers.[3] The spread of labor militancy was confirmed by the large number of strikes and labor disputes which occurred between 1944 and 1952 among sugar workers, textile workers, railway workers, government employees, military men, and police officers. The communist movement was most successful in recruiting the leaders of the working class who were often trade union officers and skilled workers. Some rank and file members were brought into the underground by their union representatives, but the first contacts were almost always made through the leadership of the union.

After the war, when small groups of workers became interested in the revolutionary left, they either joined an underground organization outright or worked alongside it in legal front groups which sought to improve labor conditions and deepen the struggle for national independence. Fuad Mursi, one of the founders and leaders of the Egyptian Communist Party in the 1950s, explained the general role workers were asked to play by the communists:

> We were not asking workers to make a socialist revolution but
> . . . the national democratic revolution. . . . We were concentrating on the national question, getting rid of British colonialism and imperialism—not only the monarchy, the remnants of feudalism and Egyptian monopolies. . . . We were asking the workers to concentrate on the national democratic question in the field of politics and to change their working conditions in the economic field.[4]

Egyptian communists were overwhelmingly male, but the women who were involved in the movement were equally dedicated and hard working. Those women who devoted themselves to the radical cause disregarded convention. They scorned the fact that Egyptian society in the 1930s and 1940s was socially traditional, that men and women were generally separated in the private domain of the house and the more public sphere of the street.[5] They were rebelling against a society in which the family was the nucleus of the community and most decisions were expected to derive from it, where marriages were still arranged, and women were regarded as the legitimate possession of men. They resented women's limited experience with government, education, business, and professional life, and refused to accept a reality in which women, on the whole, did not exert a powerful force in society.

The inequality suffered by women was both legally and socially based. While Islamic law allowed a woman to own property, conduct business, and inherit a portion of her father's estate equal to half her brother's share, it put her at her husband's mercy in matters concerning divorce and the family. Although the vast majority of women were totally dependent on men, there were exceptions. Among intellectuals of the haute and petit bourgeoisie, the traditional way of thinking existed, but with less force. Within the more cosmopolitan world of leftist politics or in the *lycée* and the university, men and women were mingling together socially and academically, barriers were breaking down, and conventional roles were being challenged. While young, modern, emancipated Egyptian women were a small minority in 1945, they existed and some went on to become leaders of the students', women's, and leftist movements.

Women's participation in formal Egyptian politics was not new. It dated back at least to the 1919 revolution when Egyptian women protested the British occupation and demonstrated in the streets alongside male members of their families. A few women were even jailed for short periods of time because of their political activity. Groups of "gentlewomen" began a social revolution when they threw off their veils, rejected the harem, and began organizing Egypt's social services.[6] Women belonged to the Wafd Party, participated in the antifascist groups which proliferated in Egypt during the 1930s, and in the 1940s joined the budding underground communist movement.

Inge Aflatun, the well-known political activist, feminist, and gifted artist described her background and her introduction to leftist politics:

> I was born in Cairo, into a family of large landowners. Education was important and many of my family studied abroad. . . . The family spoke French which was typical of bourgeois families at the time. . . . My introduction to politics came through the social and economic conditions of the time. I was shocked by the poverty and by the differences between classes. I felt this by instinct. I began painting when I was young but I was not happy about it. . . . Then came an important event . . . in 1941 while I was still a student at the French lycée. Kamil al-Tilmisani from the Art and Liberty group who was also very poor wanted to give private art lessons. He heard about this bourgeois girl who needed a teacher. We met and agreed to terms and the lessons lasted two or three years. He opened the world to me by asking, "What is art? What is life?" . . . My art exploded at the time; I had now found painting. . . . I also began questioning and searching for solutions to questions that were raised in my studies and in my life. The dissatisfaction I felt was present in my first paintings. Even the critics commented on this, saying that the artist was in a state of revolt; some hinted that it was sexual frustration. At the lycée, I met people, discussed things, found Marxist books, was in contact with young Egyptian intellectuals. Then I became a Marxist. . . . My entrance into politics and my painting were two ways to search for my country. My Arabic language skills were not very good, so at age seventeen, I began to learn Arabic.[7]

Latifa al-Zayat, a student leader in the university in 1946 and later a writer and novelist, also recollected her communist beginnings:

> I was born in a small town overlooking the Mediterranean, Damietta, in 1924 . . . into a lower middle class or upper petty bourgeois family . . . and I came to Cairo in 1936 for my education. I began university in 1942/1943. . . . By the time I was in university, I lost all hope in the existing parties because they failed to answer the national question. I became a Marxist or a communist from a nationalist point of view. What appealed to me very much in Marxism . . . was the ethics . . . the absence of discrimination in religion, race, sex. . . . I was tired of the hypocrisy, cowardice, caution and trembling of the class I belonged to.[8]

Leftist and feminist-minded women of the 1940s became increasingly interested in and articulate about the problems affecting women in Egypt, particularly those which reflected prejudicial treatment in jobs, salaries, education, and family life. Radicalized women began to think about how they might effect improvements in the status of women in society. Activity was planned with an eye to both the domestic and international scenes. Within Egypt there were efforts to politicize women about the national question and educate them about strictly female issues. Internationally, through delegations of Egyptian women traveling abroad to conferences, the world community was to be familiarized with Egyptian social problems.

In Egypt, communist women did not work primarily through existing women's organizations, like Huda Shaarawi's Feminist Union or Fatma Nimit Rashid's Feminist Party, largely because of ideological differences that were too serious to bridge. Instead, they set up a new group in 1944–45 called the League of Women Students and Graduates from the University and Egyptian Institutes (Rabitat Fatayat al-Jamia wa al-Maahid al-Misriyya).[9] The league included some fifty women, and, although it was built on the achievements of earlier feminists, it was the first women's organization in Egypt to adopt radical views about women and women's role in a revolutionary society.[10]

From the beginning, the radical, anti-imperialist complexion of the group was apparent. A pamphlet published by the organization instructed women to

> Struggle for the widest freedoms, struggle for liberation from oppression, hunger and aggression; struggle by ourselves and for our-

selves; struggle to create a free, noble life for Egyptian women under the sovereignty of a free and noble country; struggle to realize democratic freedom which cannot arrive under the shadow of the imperialist and imperialism nor under the shadow of enslavement and exploitation.[11]

The league neither constituted itself as a political party nor aspired to become one. Although a number of the league's members became active communists, the group did not plan to recruit women into the underground movement. Instead, it conceived of itself essentially as a gathering place for young women who were interested in both the narrowly gender-oriented problems of women and the larger difficulties challenging Egypt as a nation—in particular, the struggle against British colonialism.[12] The following poem, which appeared in the league's first pamphlet, expressed the group's nationalist perspective.

> . . . To you who are among those who understand
>   what the masses of women do not understand,
> What have you done for the people and for the
>   masses of women?
> Your people who are exploited, enslaved, wounded.
> And the women of our country are degraded and
>   enslaved.
> What have you done for the people and for the
>   masses of women?
> Faith does not impair you, enthusiasm does not
>   make you destitute, and loyalty is one of
>   your qualities,
> So what has come over you?
>   . . . today we extend our hands to you.
> Extend us a hand,
> Come with us and we will realize women's goals
>   and rights.
> Come. . . . We will realize with the workers of
>   Egypt their freedom and independence.[13]

The league, however, was never able to contribute significantly to the political struggle since it existed for only a short time. It was closed down by Sidqi Pasha in July 1946, along with some dozen politically hostile groups, in a campaign to eliminate the opposition. Ismail Sidqi, who began his notable political career as a supporter of

Saad Zaghlul, left the Wafd to become a member of the Liberal Constitutionalist Party after 1922. After he was elected prime minister in 1930, he founded the small, relatively insignificant People's Party. Sidqi was an autocrat whose intention was to weaken the Wafd while strengthening the monarchy. He ignored constitutional rule and tampered with election laws to keep his opponents out of office. The league challenged existing social and political conventions, and in consequence, he would not allow it to exist.

The women who entered the political sphere did so while as students or after graduation, or they were the wives and sisters of men already involved. Although they were grappling with the issues of national independence and women's liberation, leftist women directed most of their efforts toward the general political front where they thought the greatest progress could be achieved. Because of Egypt's severe underdevelopment, with the bulk of women lagging far behind men politically and educationally, it was extremely difficult to build an effective national democratic women's organization. Embryonic efforts were made through the league, but most women shared the view of Latifa al-Zayat. She noted:

> It is a luxury to think of the liberation of women . . . when you see your brothers, fathers and children strangled, scorned and exploited by foreigners and local men and women. It is only when civilization reaches a certain level, that the problems of women, children and minorities become urgent. Women make the most noble contribution to the liberation of society when they embrace causes outside themselves and outside their families. . . . One of the basic teachings of Marxism is that the individual cannot be free or liberated without his society being free and liberated. Women's fight for liberation implies a fight for the liberation of society.[14]

Male and female communists came from diverse religious and ethnic backgrounds. But, in the early years of organization, the membership was largely Jewish. Jews were tied to the antifascist movement of the 1930s and almost exclusively directed the reemergence of communist activity during the war years. There are, of course, reasons why communist culture first found expression in the Egyptian Jewish community, and an examination of Egypt's Jewish minority will prove instructive.[15]

In the 1940s, the Jewish population numbered about 75,000 or

80,000 people, or about .04 or .05 percent of the total population of Egypt. Between 45 and 50 percent of this group lived in Cairo, perhaps 35 to 40 percent lived in Alexandria, while the remainder of Jews were found principally in the Canal Zone and in a few towns of Lower Egypt.[16] The Jews were not an internally homogeneous group: there were Karaites, a small separate sect living almost exclusively in Cairo; Sephardis who migrated to Egypt in the sixteenth century, originally from Spain and Portugal; Askenazis, Jews of Central and Eastern Europe, the majority of whom settled in Egypt in the nineteenth and twentieth centuries; and indigenous Egyptian Jews whose families had lived in Egypt for hundreds of years.

While many of its members were both financially and educationally impoverished, as a community the Jews claimed an inordinately high number of respectable positions in finance, commerce, industry, and the professions. As was customary for a significant number of the foreign community in Egypt, a high proportion of Jews held European citizenship. This convention dated back to the period of the "capitulations" when possession of foreign citizenship guaranteed legal, financial, and social privileges. Jews tended to become French, Italian, or British subjects which gave them advantages denied to native Egyptians.

Within the Jewish community, class and cultural differences existed. There were many poor Jews living in the Harat al-Yahud section of Cairo who were completely indistinguishable from their Muslim counterparts. With the exception of their adherence to religious belief, they ate, spoke, dressed, and lived in virtually identical ways. There were also those like Shahata Harun, a communist fellow-traveler, who was born in Cairo and who had Syrian and Egyptian grandparents.[17] Arabic was spoken at home and Shahata Harun's father, a salesman in the Jewish department store owned by Cicuriel, held Egyptian citizenship. Despite the fact that his father could hardly read or write, having left school at the age of ten, he encouraged his son's pursuit of education. Harun was sent to an academically respectable Catholic school where instruction took place in French, and later entered Cairo University's Faculty of Law where he was introduced to Islam, Islamic law, and the formal study of the Arabic language. His social circle, for the most part, was comprised of other educated Jewish youth who spoke French and looked abroad for cultural inspiration. Nevertheless, as a result of his father's advice, his own university and legal training, and the increasing politicization of his friends, he became more Egyptianized.

The cultural and intellectual world of middle- and upper-class Egyptian Jews derived from Europe and specifically from England, France, and Italy. Jews were at home when transacting international business deals in Cairo or Paris, when vacationing in Florence, or when relaxing with the novels of Flaubert. Yet, Egyptian Jews were at the same time quintessentially a people without links to a national homeland. As a result, the most basic ties of many Jews were within Egyptian society. Unlike the Greeks, French, or Italians who were organized as separate communities within the Egyptian state and lived as in an occupied country with the British troops as protectors, the Jews were more diverse. They were both of Egypt and of the foreign world outside Egypt.

Those who could trace their Egyptian ancestry back hundreds of years lived an integrated Egyptian life; they spoke Arabic and often wore the *galabiyya*.[18] The more recent immigrants clung to their European heritage, linguistically, culturally, and psychologically. Because of their foreign origins and class differences, many were dissociated from the Egyptian people and their way of life. Jews, then, fell into two categories—those identifying with Egypt and those detached from it. As Raymond Stambouli, an Egyptian Jew who lived in Cairo until the end of World War II remarked, the Jew was the "honest broker," sometimes with Egyptians and sometimes with foreigners.[19]

Not until 1936, with the signing of the Anglo-Egyptian Treaty, did middle- and upper-class Egyptian Jews become significantly aware of the growing nationalist movement in the country. The expectation of impending change in Egypt led Jews to a serious assessment of their future positions and their security.[20] They believed that something important was happening in Egypt. Egyptian self-confidence was growing and the desire for national independence intensifying. The British, at some future point, would be bound or forced to recognize nationalist aspirations and withdraw their occupation forces. The 1936 Treaty was but the most recent and visible sign that the Egyptians were moving toward ruling their own country.

The question for Jews at this time was "What would happen to our sons in Egypt?" Several answers were posed, thus dividing Jews into three categories. Those in the first group believed that young Jews should learn Arabic, study in Egyptian rather than foreign schools, become more intimately involved in Egyptian affairs, and participate in Egyptian domestic politics. They were encouraged to break from a past in which foreigners exerted little influence in the political process and voiced few opinions on local politics. They were to alter their assumption that there was no place for Jews inside mainstream or radical political parties. For Jews contemplating this alternative a contradiction arose: how should they handle the traditional wisdom which stated that Jews as a group do not mix in local politics? This predicament was a particularly sensitive one for young people who felt the divisions in the community most profoundly.

For Jews contemplating their prospects, a second option was to emigrate from Egypt to Palestine and help build a Zionist state.[21] While a minority of the Jewish population advocated this trend, Zionism was generally an alien ideology to most Egyptian Jews.

The third choice to consider was emigration to one or another European country where acceptance and assimilation were anticipated: France and, after World War II, Italy were favored havens. A significant percentage of the Jewish community selected this option and left Egypt during the 1940s.

If 1936 was a turning point in the Egyptian political domain, it was also an important juncture for the Jewish community. At that time, Jews were trying to understand the international situation — the rise of fascism in Europe and the political divisions of right and left. The cosmopolitan community was schooled in foreign languages. Its members read foreign newspapers, listened to foreign radio broadcasts and, in particular, were concerned about the encroachment of the fascist campaign. Amidst international aggression and the threat to their own community, Jews were trying to locate a place for themselves in an unsettled and increasingly hostile world.

The exposure to foreign culture through language should not be underestimated. Literate in at least French and English, the cosmopolitan Jews were conversant with Enlightenment philosophy and aware of the ideas and movements current abroad. They read the works of Rousseau and Voltaire, the novels of Victor Hugo and Alexander Dumas.[22] Political and historical materials and Marxist works were read in English and French. Since some were unavailable in Egypt, they were procured either by mail or bought when traveling abroad. Aime Beresi, a communist during the early 1940s, stated, "Jews were on the front line of intellectual development" and this was at least partially attributable to their acquaintance with European language and culture.[23] For intellectual Jews, the cultural life and ideological atmosphere in which they lived and to which they alluded derived from Europe where the left was conducting antifascist activity.

Jewish intellectuals were captivated by the events and movements of the day: the Spanish civil war, the Ethiopian war, the Popular Front in France, and, later, the battle of Stalingrad, all of which were inextricably linked to the development of fascism in the West and beyond. For Jews in Egypt, support for the antifascist cause was a matter of self-preservation. This was especially true as Hitler's power increased and no country seemed safe from the fascist threat.

As Jews perceived their position in society growing increasingly tenuous, the political activity of some intensified. Support for the antifascist cause expanded and matured, with the result that the renewal of Marxism in the latter 1930s became tied almost exclusively to a small sector of the Jewish community. Out of a population of some 75,000 Jews in Egypt in 1946, only about 500 to 700 were communists, constituting at most one percent of the community.[24] However, compared to the percentage of native indigenous Egyptians involved with communism, the Jewish presence in the movement was highly disproportionate.

What caused this number of Jews to sympathize with Marxism was political indignation at the British occupation and a sense of social conscience in regard to the misery and injustice suffered by the mass of Egyptian society. Jews who were influenced by the democratic and socialist ideas being imported from Europe felt disgraced by and somewhat responsible for the inequities in Egypt. Indeed, they were very deeply affected by the inherent contradictions in their society.[25] But there was another, perhaps less conscious explanation for their leftist predisposition. Espousing radical ideas was a way for Jews to build into the majority culture. It was a path toward self-identification with the larger Egyptian society and a means of absolving themselves of the bourgeois traditions from which, for the most part, they emerged. If Jews advocated an internationalist ideology like Marxism, perhaps it was because they were trying to find self-realization and a place for themselves in a society in which they were a minority. It was only within the realm of internationalism that this could be achieved. Radicalized Jews condemned narrow ethnic sectarianism and stressed the importance of social class and its impact on mass culture. As a distinct group, Jews were most prominent in the Marxist movement during the war years; after 1946 a serious effort was made to Egyptianize the ranks.

From the outset the Egyptian communists confronted serious organizational problems. Although they were filled with enthusiasm, they suffered from a limited knowledge of Egyptian political realities and Marxist theory. They launched their formal militant activity in small, autonomous, clandestine groups limited to their closest associates and friends. Each association, undisciplined and conspiratorial, was comprised of members who perceived their former allies in the antifascist and democratic movement as potential enemies. Every leading personality, though familiar with his own small community of fellow dissidents, was nonetheless suspicious of the intentions, aspirations, and goals of presumptively antagonistic competitors. This highly sensitive and skeptical behavior shaped the content of the clandestine organizations. As a result, the second wave of communist activity in Egypt began in a haphazard fashion, and a labyrinth of political organizations emerged, some significant, others transient or inconsequential. The most notable feature of the movement, which also proved devastating, was that the divisiveness so evident from the very early years was never adequately addressed or entirely overcome.

Communists were distrustful of one another and unprepared, either politically or temperamentally, to search out and combine with sympathizers from competitive Marxist groups. Since there was almost no experience at the beginning of the movement of internal party struggle, the idea of banding together with others holding even slightly divergent ideological or organizational views was considered opportunism. Thus, instead of forming a united communist organization with admittedly diverse elements committed to working out their differences inside a corporate structure, the Egyptian communist movement of the 1940s began divided into a number of disconnected and sometimes antagonistic groups.

3

The Historical Development of the Egyptian Communist Movement, 1942–1947

Wartime Politics

THE MARXIST TREND which surfaced in Egypt in the early 1940s can be seen as a product of three concrete phenomena: the international situation marked by the rise of fascism and the military triumphs of the Soviet Union during World War II; the burning issue of the British occupation and the ineffective response to it by the mainstream political parties, in particular the Wafd; and the gross socioeconomic inequality.

The antifascist and democratic movement raging in Europe from the mid-1930s had a pronounced impact on young left radicals in Egypt. Politically and philosophically, Egyptian militants were inspired by the lofty ideals of democracy, social justice, and freedom. They supported the Allied cause, fighting the fascist threat in any way possible, whether through distributing antifascist literature or engaging in more direct political organization.

As the Nazi campaign triggered something in the minds of the activists, so too did the ultimately victorious example of the Soviet armies. In fact, the Soviet Union was but a blank space on the world map to most Egyptians before the battle of Stalingrad firmly implanted its image on the Egyptian leftist consciousness. "Just as the October victories created Chinese Communism, so Stalingrad gave birth to Egyptian Communism," stated an Egyptian communist bulletin.[1] The Soviet Union was applauded by radical Egyptians because it was triumphant, respectable and, not incidentally, untainted by imperialist adventures in the Arab Middle East. It was, moreover, hoped that alliance with the Soviet Union would contribute to the end of imperialist domination in Egypt. Not accidentally, the first communist groups were formed after the successes of the Red Army were widely publicized by the Allied forces.

Political frustrations in Egypt were connected directly with the British occupation. The 1936 Anglo-Egyptian Treaty had not only proven incomplete, but in fact had given a legal rationale to the occupation. Consequently, the British presence was still deeply felt in social, economic, and political matters. World War II, moreover, allowed the British to consolidate their position militarily through the increase of troops stationed in the country, economically through the control of imports and exports and the establishment of the Middle East Supply Center, and politically through the forced imposition of al-Nahhas Pasha as Prime Minister on February 4, 1942.[2] The events of February 4 struck a blow to the Wafd from which it never recovered. It lost its hegemonic nationalist standing in the country and the population as a whole never forgave al-Nahhas for the national humiliation to which he acquiesced. Britain's coercive action confirmed that Egypt's independence was nothing more than a sham.

The absence of national independence produced social and political unrest. While the rising discontent gradually weakened the old order, the nontraditional and oppositional parties were strengthened. Organizationally, the communists, the Muslim Brotherhood, and Young Egypt were the beneficiaries of this increasing dissatisfaction. Separately, they participated in anti-British activity and gave new energy to the nationalist movement. Simultaneously, their complaints were becoming clearer, as they protested staggering inflation, anguishing shortages, increasing joblessness, and unfulfilled promises of national self-determination. They grew more combative as conventional political forces in Egypt were undermined and conventional policies were denounced. Disenchanted, sections of the population became radicalized in response to perpetually stalemated negotiations with the British, a discredited monarchy, and the political compromises made by the Wafd.

Once considered aggressively patriotic and incorruptible, Wafdist leaders lost the political and social status that heretofore had elevated them above the semifeudal heads of opposing political parties. Makram Ubayd's exposure of corruption at the very pinnacle of the Wafd, involving al-Nahhas and his wife, was symptomatic of the party's loss of status. In addition, the social composition of the membership was changing: newer members of the Wafd included sons of the great families, large factory owners, and merchants who were closer to the

Palace and more prone to compromise with the British.[3] In essence, as part of society was becoming more radical, the leading political party became more conservative.

The radicalism of the times produced a new generation which expressed oppositional political views and social beliefs. While the old order was certainly not yet dead, the emerging dissidents had less and less in common with the established system. In particular, groups of youth in schools and universities, industrial workers, and city folk who were no longer unconditionally committed to older political bodies, felt confident enough to set up new groups which were more representative of their ideas.[4] The militants, who began their activity during the war, found a relatively suitable political atmosphere in which to work since the occupation forces generally turned a blind eye to communist organization in the hope of making use of its anti-fascist influence.[5]

In the early 1940s, four separate communist groups were organized in Egypt. Three were significant and merit discussion: the Egyptian Movement for National Liberation (EMNL), Iskra, and the New Dawn. The fourth group, People's Liberation, was founded by Marcel Israel, an Egyptian Jew holding Italian citizenship. It was a primitive short-lived organization known for its stubborn antireligious stand. Its theory was that in order to be a communist, one must be an atheist and preach atheism in Egypt. Marcel Israel was linked with some of the high intellectuals leaning toward Trotskyism for whom the stand of atheism was not heretical. The group's brief existence left no impression on the political life of the country. The other groups were, however, more influential.

The Egyptian Movement for National Liberation

The Egyptian Movement for National Liberation (al-Haraka al-Misriyya lil Taharrur al-Watani) was founded by Henri Curiel in 1943. Curiel remains a controversial figure in the history of Egyptian communism. He was recently described as "a bogus Gandhi who always appeared in short pants, even in December and January,"[6] as "a frail-looking intellectual who would seem more at home in the Bodleian than in the factories in the Cairo suburbs,"[7] as "an efficient revolutionary who gave his life for the ideas he was fighting and working for."[8] Curiel was loved and hated; admired and denounced. While there is certainly nothing approaching a consensus of opinion about Henri Curiel, he was indisputably the leading figure in the whole of the Egyptian communist movement of the 1940s. Who was this man?

On September 13, 1914, Henri Curiel was born into a rich Jewish Egyptian family. He was third generation Egyptian on his father's side. His mother was from Constantinople. His father, Daniel, was a banker, businessman, and landowner who owned property in Mansuriyya in the province of Giza, in Minufiyya, and in Qalyub. Curiel received a European education, first at the Jesuit school in Cairo and later at the École Française de Droit where he received a B.A. degree in Law. When Curiel reached age twenty-one in 1935, he took Egyptian nationality, relinquishing the right to his father's Italian passport and thereby eschewing the privilege of foreign citizenship.

Curiel's origins pointed to anything but communism. He was "foreign," knew little Arabic, was very rich, and had few meaningful links with the indigenous population—one might have thought him unable to develop bonds with the mass of Egyptians. Yet, he became a revolutionary committed to changing the structure of Egyptian society.

Both from his own writings and through his associates' comments, a picture of Curiel emerges. He was deeply touched by the Egyptian national movement and impatient with the condition of life prevailing in the country. From 1936, with the signing of the Anglo-Egyptian Treaty which he perceived as a national defeat allowing Egypt only limited independence, he began reading Marxist texts in the hope of finding answers to Egypt's nagging problems. By the early years of the war, he believed he understood the root causes and adverse consequences of inequality in Egypt. Paradoxically, perhaps, as a beneficiary of Egypt's class system, Curiel was acutely aware of the contradictions inherent in a society where the vast majority lived in wretched poverty, while a tiny minority enjoyed the lion's share of the country's wealth. For Curiel, Marx not only spoke to economic issues but also addressed national and political problems. Hardly immune to the realities of international events, Curiel, a Jew, was both shocked and roused by the impending threat of world fascism. These concerns impelled him to act. Because of his outspoken attitudes and controversial behavior he was considered reckless by the elders of the Jewish community for voluntarily involving himself in local politics. Disregarding their advice and warnings, he became active in a campaign which was to lead him on a collision course with the police, his family, and the politically conscious members of the Egyptian political arena.

Always conscious of his social background, he stated before the prosecution in the 1946 court case in which he and others were being tried by Ismail Sidqi's government for the crime of being a communist:

> People say that I am the son of a millionaire. In spite of this I see that it is necessary to limit land holdings and if a time comes when landownership will be restricted, I will . . . agree to limit the size of my holdings. . . . We need to make some progress in this direction. . . . For me, personally, I am one of the exceptions in the sense that I do not see that my direct interests should halt the way of general progress.[9]

Henri Curiel was intimately involved in every phase of the Egyptian communist movement until September 1950, when he was arrested, transported secretly to Port Said, put on an Italian ship, and exiled to Italy. In 1951 he arrived in France where he lived, semilegally, as a political refugee and worked on behalf of revolutionary causes throughout the world. He was particularly involved in the struggle for Algerian independence, and as a fraternal gesture he gave his mother's villa in Cairo to the new Algerian government to use as its embassy. He was also involved in trying to organize a dialogue between the Israelis, Palestinians, and Egyptians in an effort to establish a working group dedicated to peace in the Middle East. On May 4, 1978, Henri Curiel was assassinated by still unknown persons.

Samuel Bardell, a communist in the British army during World War II, and at that time a close associate of Curiel's in Cairo, attended his friend's funeral. He noted:

> There were over a thousand people present, young, middle-aged and old. . . . There were official representatives from the French Communist Party, from the French Socialist Party, from the Israeli Communist Party and from the illegal Egyptian Communist Party; but there were also representatives from the Algerian government and from the Catholic Church in France.
>
> They were of many races and seemed of all nationalities and they were there to pay their last respects to a man who left a lasting impression on all who met him, yet who was condemned by the official communist parties of France and Britain (although he had founded the Egyptian Communist Party) and who, though a man of peace, had been linked with terrorists like Carlos by scurrilous journalists. The French police were also present in large numbers, both in uniform and plain clothes. French TV was there

and numerous journalists with cameras and recorders, jostling around the widow and the mourners, noting down the speeches and tributes that were listened to in silence.[10]

Well before the official establishment of the EMNL, Curiel began plotting the course he would pursue in his effort to found a communist organization. As a first step, he tried to bring Marxist theory to the Egyptians.[11] According to Curiel, few people in Egypt understood the meaning and breadth of communism. His aim was to get books, have them translated, and pass them on to those he thought best able to effect change in the society.[12] In 1941, he opened al-Midan bookstore in central Cairo with money provided by his well-to-do father. Marxist books were imported from England, the United States, France, and the Soviet Union. A host of newspapers, pamphlets, and a variety of foreign publications were sold. William Handley, labor attaché in the American Embassy in Cairo later in the decade, described what he saw during a visit to the bookshop.

> There is a heavy preponderance of literature on the Soviet Union and pictures of Stalin were prominently displayed. Among the books were several editions printed in English and French on Soviet subjects, as for example, "Soviet Unions and Soviet Influence" and "Cultural Work of Soviet Unions." Moreover, there was one entire section devoted to Arabic books, many of which had obviously Russian slanted covers, for example, pictures of Stalin and what appeared to be Russian trade union representatives. . . . On the door of the shop were several copies of French communist newspapers. There were many books on American labor, but these books have been written by American communists, for example, Foster, and emphasize the plight of American labor in the hands of reactionary capitalism, as well as the deplorable working conditions in America.[13]

The bookstore served as a meeting place for Egyptian intellectuals, allowed Egyptians to make contact with foreign radicals, including members of European military forces stationed in Egypt during the war, and offered a forum for discussions of social and political issues. Henri Curiel served as a mediator of European ideology to Egyptians and the bookstore provided many with their introduction to Marxist literature.

During the Second World War, Curiel began trying to determine, concretely, how to build a party. He set out by studying the practices of foreign communist parties and by trying personally to assimilate the theories of Marxism. In addition, he made efforts to meet the survivors of the first Egyptian Communist Party. From the old-timers he learned that the party was founded by the Communist International and the Egyptian members themselves knew little about communism and less about the process of setting up a communist group. Although the cadres were full of good will, they were easily destroyed because they had no party structure, no notion of how a cell functioned, and very little theoretical knowledge.[14]

Unlike the communists of the early 1920s, the people active in the 1940s were neither products of the Comintern nor Comintern representatives. In fact, in contrast to Syria, Palestine, and Iraq, which had relations with the Soviet Union, Egyptian communists were peculiarly unaffiliated. As Rifaat al-Said stated, "when a quarrel arose [in the Fertile Crescent], the 'headmaster' came with his stick and determined who was wrong and who was right. There was no 'headmaster' in Egypt."[15] Essentially, the Russians were skeptical about the minority Jewish leadership of the Egyptian left and wary of the lack of unity in the movement. Ultimately, the Soviet Union simply did not wish to commit itself to one faction in an anarchist leftist movement. Later on, Egyptian communists regretted the absence of international ties and in the mid-1950s sought ways to remedy this deficiency.

Curiel was deeply aware of the absence of Soviet recognition. But since he could not expect Russian endorsement or aid, he set out to find the Egyptian road to communism. The first problem he confronted was the form the Egyptian organization should take. He puzzled over whether conditions in the early 1940s would allow for the establishment of an Egyptian communist party, or whether Marxists needed to proceed gradually and first set up a communist organization. Because he feared that launching a party too quickly without a strong base to support it would cause it to fall as rapidly as the first Egyptian Communist Party, Curiel decided to move slowly and begin by creating a radical organization with a Marxist membership and philosophy.

Although Curiel was deeply influenced by the Soviet Union, he was able to distance himself from it when he deemed it appropriate. For example, he did not follow the conventional Soviet format for organization. While at its top, the EMNL did consist of a central secretariat made up of the group's four leading members, and at the bottom the rank and file were recruited into cells of three or four cadres, he set up sections in between these levels. The sections represented military men, students, those of a common national origin, workers, those from the provinces, those from particular neighborhoods, women, intellectuals, and professionals.

When Curiel began meeting with his closest friends, they struggled over how to establish the nucleus of a party in Egypt. Raymond Stambouli recalled:

> We opened the books of Lenin and Stalin to find out what is a cell? What is the work of a cell? How is it organized? What is the link between cells? What is the political bureau, the secretariat, security, clandestinity? What is the attitude toward religion? . . . If someone said he was a communist, we took him and pumped him for details of communist activity. . . . There was a mass of strenuous effort to understand things, the smallest things, with no help from anyone. . . . We tried to find solutions to problems by day to day work.[16]

The first people Curiel gathered around him were trusted companions: a few Jews (among whom were Joe Matalon and David Nahum); a few Egyptian intellectuals (among whom were Muhammad Zaki Hashim and Tahsin al-Misri); a few Egyptian workers (Sid Sulayman Rifai was one); and Sudanese and Nubians (for example, Abdu Dhahab).[17] The group expanded from this core.

Curiel was never interested in recruiting mainly intellectuals or minorities; rather he concentrated his efforts on establishing links with the more disenfranchised members of society. To Curiel, the EMNL was required to find practical answers to mundane questions: what to do in the province, the village, the trade union, the factory, the school. From the beginning, there was worker activity in the EMNL, first in the Shubra al-Khayma factory complex which employed some 17,000 workers, then in Alexandria, and later in Mahalla al-Kubra where 27,000 more employees worked. Although the working class did not become an independent political force until World War II, it was not altogether surprising that its downtrodden conditions of existence provided fertile ground for communist agitation. Even the British Embassy labor counselor was compelled to comment on the abhorrent circumstances prevalent among Egyptian workers. M. Audsley wrote:

The Egyptian workers live in unhealthy and overcrowded dwellings —they are so overcrowded in many areas that the workers occupy the dwellings in shifts as in a factory; they sleep in the streets and in any odd corner; servants and their families sleep under staircases, in sheds and in gardens or in quarters in the more modern buildings which are often not sanitary. Their nutrition is usually inadequate and lacking in food values. Their health conditions are appalling and the provisions for dealing with diseases are totally inadequate. . . . Their level of wages is below the subsistence standard, e.g. in 1942 it was calculated officially that to keep a family of six at the lowest standard of subsistence a wage of the equivalent of £E4.8 per month was required, but the average wage at the time was assessed at £E3 per month. Their clothing is inadequate and frequently unclean and disease ridden. . . . There is no unemployment insurance, no provision for old age and similar state benefits. . . .[18]

The spate of strikes which erupted between 1945 and 1952 were protests against increased unemployment, declining real wages, and general poverty. Actually, during these times of crisis, working class militants demanded more than limited economic redress—though this in itself was justified. They also called for an end to imperialist control of Egypt and the relaxation of landlords' feudal hold on property.

Muhammad Shatta, a textile worker in Shubra al-Khayma, was recruited by the EMNL. His presence was singularly significant because it was through Shatta that the EMNL established its presence in the Shubra area, distributed communist leaflets urging trade union militancy, and participated in strike activity. Shubra al-Khayma was the scene of continuous labor disturbances during 1945. By late December of that year these disturbances reached a climax when between 5000 and 7000 workers staged a walkout. The strike was significant because of the presence of communist activists and sympathizers— led by Shatta—and because of the radical nature of the workers' demands. No longer content to accept low wages and poor working conditions, labor showed a new level of determination to hold out for the rights it believed were its due. Workers' militancy and communist infiltration into one of Egypt's largest industrial complexes alarmed the Ministry of the Interior which, after the end of the strike, ordered wholesale arrests of all workers suspected of communist tendencies. This, however, did little to lessen working class militancy which continued to trouble the factory owners in Shubra al-Khayma, and members of the government as well, throughout the year 1946 and indeed for the remainder of the decade.

In order to capture and channel the trade union combativeness at the beginning of 1945, the EMNL founded the Congress of the Union of Workers of Public Companies and Institutions. A federation of shop-keepers, tram employees, and workers from the cinema, textile, and electrical industries, its purpose was to assist the party in organizing and educating workers. It came into being in response to international labor developments, most notably the establishment of the World Fed-eration of Trade Unions (WFTU), and it sent representatives to Paris to participate in the WFTU's first meeting. Traveling to Paris were Muhammad Abd al-Halim, president of the Union of Egyptian Workers at the Egyptian press, David Nahum, vice-president of the Union of Workers of Commercial Stores, and Murad al-Qaliyubi, president of the Union of Cinema Workers. Taking part in an international labor event was an important milestone for these Egyptian trade unionists because it gave them the feeling of belonging to a nationally tran-scendent movement with a long tradition of fairness and equity.

Since the Congress was designed to counteract restrictive mea-sures imposed upon the labor syndicates by the government and to combat the arrest of labor leaders, the group was carefully monitored by the authorities. When, for example, it scheduled a mass meeting on May 1, 1946 to coordinate the diverse affairs of Egyptian labor, Prime Minister Sidqi prevented the meeting from taking place.[19] Still determined to continue their activity, a number of unionists met together on the same date and decided to cancel the Congress of the Union of Workers of Public Companies and Institutions and form in its place a new body called the Congress of the Union of Egyptian Workers. Husayn Kazim was appointed secretary-general. Only labor unions were invited to join this Congress and every union was per-mitted to keep its internal autonomy as far as organization was con-cerned on the condition that it did not contradict the general pur-poses and rules of the Congress. The new body sent a memo to Prime Minister Sidqi in which it made the following demands:

- to realize total evacuation of the British from the Nile Valley
- to apply the same standards and labor laws to all Egyptian workers
- to combat unemployment by government efforts to prevent fac-tories from closing
- to prohibit the firing of workers from their jobs

- to release from jail those workers arrested for their patriotic and
    union activity
- to institute a forty-hour work week without affecting the pres-
    ent level of wages
- to have one weekend holiday for all workers
- to consider the first day of May Labor Day for all workers.[20]

The Congress insisted that the demands be met by June 9, 1946, as a means of demonstrating its purpose. When the government took no action, the Congress called a general strike on June 10, but because some workers were in the process of negotiating with the Ministry of Social Affairs and because of a general lack of strength the strike was postponed. Even after the Congress allied with another communist inspired labor group led by Muhammad Yusuf al-Mudarrik, Taha Saad Uthman, and Mahmud al-Askari, and announced a second strike on June 25, sufficient support could not be generated and this effort also ended in failure.

The Congress of the Union of Egyptian Workers was founded in order to influence labor union activity and to join in the defense of working-class interests. It was the EMNL's intention to tighten the links between the various trade union groups in the hope of establishing a united trade union movement and, in the process, to politicize a restless working class. By this time, however, the party had penetrated at best only the leaderships of several trade unions. If Marxism supplied the workers with slogans and encouraged them to strike for the realization of their demands, it was not yet able to turn rank and file union members into activists for the communist cause.[21]

Trade union leaders affiliated with the EMNL were also instrumental in facilitating the still very limited contacts between the organization and the peasantry. Through leaders such as Muhammad Hamza, for example, working in Mahalla al-Kubra, initial political links were formed with interested individuals in the villages surrounding the industrial area. In general, since many of the workers in Mahalla, Shubra al-Khayma, and Alexandria were of peasant origin, and their personal ties to their ancestral villages were still strong, their direct efforts to recruit relatives or friends were sometimes effective. While it may be said that workers had one foot in the factory and one foot in the village, that they were half urban worker and half villager, they were still directly tied to their birthplace and maintained close personal relations with the inhabitants.[22] Still, the EMNL could make use of these bonds only to a limited extent. It was the Democratic

Movement of National Liberation (DMNL) which superseded the EMNL, that capitalized on these links by concentrating more of its human resources on recruitment among peasants.

One of the members of the EMNL, Abdu Dhahab, established a connection with Sudanese and Nubian Azharites and through them made contact with Egyptian Azharites and Sudanese living in Egypt. A small but significant group of Sudanese nationals was recruited into the organization. The EMNL put forward a radical solution to the colonial situation in Sudan. While the established political parties called for "One Nile, One Kingdom, One King in the Nile Valley," the communists of the EMNL appealed for national self-determination for the Sudanese and raised the slogan, "Common struggle between the Egyptian and Sudanese people against a common [British] enemy." Two legal newspapers which the EMNL sponsored and supported, *Hurriyat al-Shuub* (The Freedom of the People) and *Umdurman*, propagated these views.

The Sudanese who became communists, in fact, later returned to Sudan and set up the Sudanese Movement for National Liberation (SMNL), in 1947. Because most of the leaders of the SMNL were educated and trained inside the EMNL or the DMNL, the success of the Sudanese group in organizing the working class and becoming a major force in the society has been considered one of the EMNL's most important achievements.

Nubians were also connected to the EMNL and they numbered about seventeen in the mid-1940s.[23] Led by Mubarrak Abdu Fadl and Muhammad Khalil Qassim, they played an important role in the national struggle in the hopes of preventing the British from separating Nubia from Egypt.[24]

Party efforts were made to recruit students from al-Azhar. Many of those enrolled at the Islamic university were from humble rural backgrounds. After the creation of the modern secular university, the Egyptian educational system was bifurcated. While the more affluent classes sent their sons to the secular institution, the only educational opportunity open to the poor was at al-Azhar, where they were entitled to free education, a very small living allowance, food, and modest lodgings.

A small group of poor village Azharites, perhaps numbering about fifteen, allied itself with the EMNL. The Azharites recruited into the organization obviously knew the party had a Marxist orientation, but they did not perceive the group as atheist. This was because Curiel was never doctrinaire about the religious question and was content to detach religion from Marxism. The EMNL understood men of religion and tried to use Islam in the service of the radical cause. Abd al-Rahman al-Thaqafi, himself a communist Azharite, pursued the idea of studying Islam as a militant religious philosophy which protested against both imperialism and internal exploitation. His two books, *Islam and Communism* and *The First Revolutionary in Islam*, put forth his ideas.

Soon after its establishment the EMNL also made inroads into the army through Ibrahim al-Attar, Jamal Salim, and Salah Salim, and in the air force through Uthman Fawzi.[25] A group of noncommissioned officers in the air force were recruited first. These were semieducated and increasingly class conscious men who, though they were graduated from the mechanical air force school, lived the life of the common soldier—always at odds with their superiors and with virtually no hope of advancement.

Fuad Habashi was characteristic of this group. Born in Zifta in Gharbiyya province, he came from a Coptic family of craftsmen and small landowners. After completing his early education in the provinces, Habashi attended and graduated from the School of Aircraft Mechanics. A sympathizer with the EMNL, he carried the organization's propaganda to the military mechanics, maintenance workers, clerks, musicians, and even to the civilian workers employed by the forces. Habashi's importance to the communists lay in his willingness and ability to organize prospective leftists. He focused attention on the national liberation movement, on the achievements of democracy, and on the need for increased wages inside the military, issues with which his associates could identify.

In the military, a form of the class struggle was being played out between soldiers, noncommissioned officers, and officers, with the middle group sympathetic to the plight of the lowly soldier. The EMNL, aware of the divisions in the military, tried to capitalize on them by emphasizing the inequalities which were built into the system of recruitment and advancement. When the party first began organizing, it captured a small audience by putting forward a very basic program which concentrated on the national liberation of Egypt, the right of noncommissioned officers to be promoted, and the necessity of improved conditions for the common soldier who, at the time, was paid a mere fifty-four piasters a month and lived on an almost exclusive diet of lentils. In contrast, the non-commissioned officers received £E3 a month salary.[26]

In order to develop the diverse recruits ideologically and politically, the first cadre school of the EMNL was established in 1943. It convened at Curiel's farmhouse in the countryside at Mansuriyya in the province of Giza. The purpose of the cadre school was to prepare the most promising members of the EMNL for the tasks awaiting them in the movement. About twenty-five students attended the first session. During the course of one week, the group typically participated in workshops and heard lectures focusing on the history of Egypt, the geography of Egypt, dialectical materialism, political economy, and the method of historical materialism. There were also short courses on the elements of Marxism and analyses of the class structure of Egypt. Discussions were held focusing on the equality of the sexes, education, the U.S.S.R. and the history of its Communist Party, and Marxist philosophy.[27] Future cadre courses were planned, with the purpose of inaugurating new members or raising the level of information of the more seasoned veterans. Consistently, the themes raised in the cadre courses included the most immediate issues for the EMNL: the nationalist problem, the Sudanese question, class inequality, and the Egyptianization and proletarianization of the movement.

Regarding national liberation, the EMNL militantly disagreed with the mainstream parties' emphasis on continued negotiations with the British to gain independence. The negotiation process, which had a long and discouraging history in Egypt, failed to realize the nationalists' demands for military, political, and economic freedom. Therefore, the communists insisted on devising alternative and radical policies to contend with the continued occupation: the abrogation of all bilateral treaties and the unconditional eviction of the British from the Nile Valley were two nonnegotiable requirements.

Although the revolutionary left took national liberation as its primary aim, it never ignored the material plight of poor Egyptians. Theorists of the EMNL asserted that problems such as poverty, sickness, or ignorance could not be combated separately. Indeed, the inequities built into the system needed to be changed by changing society itself.

Proletarianization and Egyptianization were two of the most basic goals of the EMNL. According to its leaders, recruitment of workers was essential to the growth and development of the party. It was through workers of local origin that the mood of the country could be felt and the ideas of change realized. In keeping with classic Marxist philosophy, they believed that the working class, in association with other radical groups in society, would accomplish revolutionary transformation. The goal of proletarianization was only partially realized since the organization successfully penetrated only the leadership of the trade union movement.

The concept of Egyptianization was brought forward in the early 1940s when there was a disproportionately large number of Jewish communists active in the country. That a majority of the EMNL leadership was of minority origin made the organization's emphasis on recruiting Egyptians a particularly radical one. From the beginning, Henri Curiel contended that the essence of the movement had to be Egyptian before it could realistically win over the popular classes. Since there was an unremitting trend toward increased Egyptian control over the affairs of the country, all forces in society would have to recognize this current. The EMNL hoped to share in this transition and help shape the course of events. The policy of Egyptianization was consciously followed and although the central committee still contained a disproportionate number of cosmopolitan Jews, the base of the organization was predominantly Egyptian.

The organization embraced what it termed a "national democratic" line, meaning essentially that it supported national liberation from occupation and the inauguration of a truly democratic system. The leadership asserted that it was important not to overplay the party's communist character, not to come forward at an inauspicious time in a hostile environment and announce its goals, but rather to concentrate on organizing sympathizers around significant but moderate issues upon which agreement could be readily reached.[28] Therefore, in an effort to build the movement and popularize its ideas, the focus was on themes which could ignite the imaginations and unite the differences of a varied group of people. National independence and a just system of government were two propositions which were not likely to produce major disagreement.

The EMNL took the form of a radical movement with a Marxist leadership and nucleus. Curiel's idea was to establish a united front whose center was the working class but whose adherents were also members of social-democratic and reformist organizations. In that way, he hoped to attract sympathizers from both the petty and national bourgeoisie.[29]

Iskra

The second important group was Iskra, founded in 1942 or 1943 by Hillel Schwartz. The leaders of Iskra, all of Jewish origin, concentrated the greater part of their energy on recruiting among the intelligentsia. The typical member they attracted was cultured, sophisticated, well-to-do, and, until 1945, Jewish. In contrast to the EMNL, there were many more women represented in Iskra. Its cosmopolitan membership was accustomed to social activity with women and had little difficulty working with them in the political movement.

Members of Iskra were recruited through the extended family or through networks of friends developed in the *lycée*, the university, or the cultural and political clubs of the day. One such avenue was the House of Scientific Research (Dar al-Abhath al-Ilmiyya), founded as a legal front group for Iskra in 1944. The surface purpose of the club was to disseminate cultural information among the members and to popularize radical views of social justice. In reality, and on a deeper level, it acquainted people with communist ideas and doctrine under the veil of scientific and cultural research. The society comprised some three hundred members of whom about fifty were young women students and college graduates.[30]

The programs of the House of Scientific Research attracted the intellectually curious and sometimes converted the politically active into communist sympathizers, fellow travelers, or even organized political militants. The group provided the atmosphere of a community where like-minded people congregated. This was important because it demonstrated that individual leftists were not alone in their nonconformist thinking. In fact, the more often people attended meetings, discussed issues of interest, learned from their contemporaries, and socialized, the more absorbed they became in leftist analysis. In the meantime, Iskra publicized its ideas and attracted new members into the organization.

The House published a monthly periodical that contained independent research as well as reproductions of the lectures initially delivered at formal meetings. These publications took the form of booklets of about fifty pages and were distributed to the members and visitors free of charge. Likewise during the sessions, copies of the left-wing magazines *Umdurman, al-Talia,* and *al-Fajr al-Jadid* were on sale, together with books written by communists or those with radical tendencies.[31]

Among the books published by the House was *The Muslim Brotherhood in the Balance* (al-Ikhwan al-muslimun fi al-mizan) by Muhammad Hasan Ahmad. This book, of which 6000 copies were printed, expressed Iskra's views of the Muslim Brotherhood: the organization was identified as fascist in outlook and as a potentially dangerous competitor. It was criticized for spreading divisive Islamic propanganda the aim of which was to separate Muslims, Copts, and Jews, and for weakening the nationalist movement against imperialism by refusing to participate in joint activity with other political groups. Moreover, it was condemned for diffusing the anticapitalist opposition by urging Muslim workers to cooperate with Muslim industrialists because of religious communality.

Passing through the House were numbers of people who later became the crème de la crème of Egypt's intelligentsia. It was through lectures, discussions, and readings offered by the body that a generation of leftists received their early political education. It was also through the House that the gap between the cosmopolitan foreigners in Iskra and the Egyptian intellectuals was bridged.[32] The House of Scientific Research was closed down on July 11, 1946, upon Prime Minister Sidqi's orders.

Another fertile ground for attracting members to Iskra was the university. Sensing the mood of the students during and after the war, the organization stressed the emotive political issues of national liberation and antiimperialism. As students became increasingly active in the nationalist campaign to free Egypt from its colonialist yoke, these were inspiring causes. Many thoughtful students found in Iskra a way of expressing their frustration with the traditional political parties, especially the Wafd, and a means through which their enthusiasm could be channeled. In the Faculties of Science, Medicine, and Law at Fuad I University, and generally within radical Cairene intellectual circles, Iskra was a visible and energetic force.

Albert Arie was a typical member of Iskra. Of Jewish origin, he could trace his family history back to the fifteenth century when his ancestors left Spain, traveled to Bulgaria, and later settled in Turkey where many generations later his father was born. Not wanting to serve in the Ottoman army, his father left Turkey just before World War I and migrated to Egypt. His mother's birthplace was Egypt.

During World War I the elder Arie opened the first sports shop in Egypt through which he distributed athletic articles to schools and social institutions and sold retail merchandise to individuals. He had social as well as business contact with Egyptians and in 1924, to the astonishment of friends in the Jewish community, he chose Egyptian nationality and gave up the privileges of a foreign passport. Albert Arie then inherited Egyptian citizenship from him.

Although both his parents shared Jewish backgrounds, they were from different upbringings and traditions. His mother was reasonably well educated; his father was virtually unschooled. While his mother's family, like many of those coming from Europe, had scant contact with Egyptians, or as they were called in this community, "Arabs," his father was fully integrated into his adopted homeland. Since his parents belonged to contrasting communities, this presented Albert Arie with a wider window from which to view the world around him.

Arie was truly a part of Egyptian society. In contrast to many of his Jewish friends, both communist and noncommunist, who began leaving Egypt first in the 1940s, then in 1952, 1956, and 1961, Arie was adamant to remain. For him, it would have been impossible to be a communist without belonging to his country: Egypt was his home and there he had to stay.

According to Hillel Schwartz, the leader of Iskra, Arie and others of his background were the people most susceptible to communist ideas: their education, culture, and inclination predisposed them to internationalist views. Reflecting his own outlook, Schwartz put forward the "stages" theory of organization in an effort to establish a broad-based party and struggle with the built-in difficulties of recruiting local Egyptians. The system worked in the following way. First, cosmopolitan minorities, in particular Jewish Egyptians, who embraced radical leftist ideas, were recruited into the organization. Second, sympathetic Egyptian intellectuals were brought into the party. The first two groups shared a certain mutuality based at least on common social background and education and so could easily work together. In the third stage, the native Egyptian intellectuals, who spoke Arabic and could relate directly with the workers, were to devote their energies to mobilizing sections of the working class. Although the cosmopolitan foreigners did recruit Egyptian intellectuals, very few workers joined the ranks of Iskra.[33]

It was not until 1945, with the rise of the national movement, that Iskra began the second period of its development and was distinguished by the entrance of local Egyptians into the group. Ibrahim al-Manistirli and Jamal Ghali were the first Egyptians to be recruited into the organization and they were soon followed by Shuhdi Atiya al-Shafii, Anwar Abd al-Malik, and others. Consistent with its intellectually oriented membership, Iskra had a rigorous theoretical bent and emphasized the education of its cadres. Sharif Hatata, of upper-middle-class, half-Egyptian, half-English origin, was among the students who were politicized in the postwar years and joined the communist movement. He remarked:

Iskra tended to appeal to a person like myself because it stressed studying and learning and reading books. This sounded good to me. I always read books when I wanted to understand something, so this seemed the right way to go about it. I didn't really choose Iskra . . . I became interested in the national movement. . . . I was contacted by people from the organization and I went to the cultural club called Dar al-Abhath. It just happened to be Iskra but it could have been anybody else. They were the people who were there at the moment.

He continued:

Everyone has a different reason for becoming attached to a political movement. For me it wasn't a matter of social interest as regards my class. It was mainly due to the fact that belonging to an upper class family with an English mother and a way of life that was somewhat isolated from the mainstream of Egyptian society, I had a need not to feel alienated. And I did have this feeling of alienation. One of the reasons why I joined the Medical College was because I thought that might be a way of becoming a part of what was happening. I had dreams of working in a rural area, helping people. Then I realized that there were more important issues than the strict medical ones—that those were only a part of other things. I didn't understand it very clearly at the time but I did realize that that was not enough. . . . Belonging to a modern set-up, it was difficult for me to join traditional political movements. It had to be something progressive, open, that wasn't traditional or fanatical. And it had to be something rational. . . . The left-wing movement was the only one that seemed to give an explanation which was valid for what was going on. . . . [For] the other groups . . . it was an emotional patriotism.[34]

Latifa al-Zayat was also part of the Iskra group and, similarly, she was energized by the liveliness of the day. When she first entered the university in 1942 she was a Wafdist sympathizer. Soon after matriculation, though, she lost all hope in the existing political parties' ability to solve the national question. Ultimately, she abandoned her Wafdist loyalties and became a Marxist for whom the nationalist cause was paramount. She recalled those days:

The years after the victory over fascism were glorious years in the history of Egypt and fruitful years. It seemed that all prospects were opened to us. Any real nationalist had to make a choice, a decision, to become a communist or a member of the Muslim Brotherhood. This was especially true after the failure of the established parties to meet the requirements of the country. Being a woman and having my temperament—that is a rebel and not a conformist—I could not join the Ikhwan. In my second year at university . . . I was asked by a woman student to attend Dar al-Abhath. I went. . . . Later, I became a member of Iskra.[35]

Iskra was organized like a pyramid. At the base of the organization were the candidates—those individuals who were secretly being groomed for membership. Iskra had a long period of candidacy during which time the prospective members were told only that they were participating in a study group. For security reasons they were not informed that they were being recruited into an underground party. Candidacy continued for about a year; then the new members were admitted into the cell.[36]

The cell was, typically, the first level of the organization where discussions and education took place and where instructions for activity were sent. Generally, the cell was composed of three members plus one person responsible for the unit in the next higher level. This next stratum, called the circle, brought together three or four cells and might have represented a school group, a cultural club, or more rarely workers in a factory. Representatives from the circles participated on a still higher level, that of the section, where separate groups of Jews, Italians, women, or students were assembled. At the top of the pyramid was the central committee, composed of a small vanguard of leaders who were in charge of the whole operation.[37]

A vehicle for airing the views of Iskra, in particular, was the newly formed newspaper, al-Jamahir (The Masses). The publication of al-Jamahir in 1946 represented a major step forward for the organization. Previously, its internal party publications were written in French and English and were geared to the cosmopolitan foreigner. Al-Jamahir was an Arabic publication reflecting the growing importance of the Egyptian cadres in the organization and the realization by the leadership that the party had to penetrate both the national movement and the majority culture. No longer was French communist literature and the works of Neruda, Aragon, and Robeson, for example, enough to capture and sustain the leftist mind. Increasingly, Egyptians were read with interest and appreciation, and the poets Kamal Abd al-Halim and Fuad Haddad became particularly popular. *Al-Jamahir* incorporated news reporting, political analysis, and cultural works, and became must reading for the whole of the leftist opposition.

The basic program of Iskra and the goals it supported were not in essence dissimilar to those of the EMNL as Sharif Hatata noted:

> If you take the political lines of the two movements and the slogans that were raised, I don't think you could distinguish at least on the surface, any big difference. I think that the differences were in how these political lines were interpreted and implemented. . . . There was a difference in social constitution and in the degree of fusion with the national movement—to which the EMNL was closer. There was a difference, therefore, in the way all problems were looked at. . . . The words were the same but what was put inside by each group was different.[38]

As early as the 1940s, the primary object of the communist movement was the achievement of national independence. Colonial rule was seen as a national indignity and a human outrage. According to the communists, only after military withdrawal took place could Egypt begin its life as a truly sovereign nation, achieve democracy, and introduce meaningful social reform. One of the issues which both groups commented on was the situation in Palestine. Interest in Palestine no doubt stemmed from the leaderships' and memberships' ethnic backgrounds: as Jews they were forced to confront the prevailing problems there. In essence, both groups opposed the immigration of Jews to Palestine and at the same time voiced their disgust with anti-Semitic incidents in Egypt and abroad. According to their analysis, since Jews and Arabs faced a common enemy—British imperialism—in Palestine, it was in their joint interests to collaborate in opposition against it.

Neither the EMNL nor Iskra had the force of strength or numbers to strike out against the British on their own. It was only with the support of at least part of the popular classes that the communists could take actions which had the potential for effectiveness. Whether it was together with the workers in Shubra al-Khayma or Mahalla al-Kubra, with students and intellectuals in the university, or in front groups set up by the left, the communist movement was dependent on the endorsement of an audience wider than itself. Because the EMNL and Iskra were small and relatively marginal organizations, their independent activity consisted mainly of distributing angry leaflets to students, professionals, and some workers, publishing critical articles in oppositional newspapers, and occasionally organizing demonstrations which were designed to stir up popular discontent at key moments in time.

The New Dawn—Popular Vanguard for Liberation

Ahmad Sadiq Saad, Yusuf Darwish, and Raymond Duwayk, whose association dated back to the antifascist activity of the late 1930s, established a separate political trend beginning in the early 1940s. Loosely called the New Dawn (al-Fajr al-Jadid) after the magazine they published together with Ahmad Rushdi Salih, it was not organized as a political party. Rather, it was a small circle of four intellectuals whose main task was to study Egyptian society and work within the existing legal organizations of workers, students, and intellectuals.[39]

Not considering the early 1940s a propitious time to establish a communist party, these militants conceived their role as one of participation in the national struggle against foreign imperialism and local conservatism. This experience, they posited, would enable them to begin to create the necessary base from which to form a party, assuming that they could federate with the vibrant sections of the workers' movement.[40] During this embryonic stage in the group's development, it practiced open and legal activity by participating in the Youth Group for Popular Culture and the Society for Spreading Modern Culture, by publishing the journal *al-Fajr al-Jadid* and the workers' newspaper *al-Damir*, and by associating with the Workers' Committee for National Liberation.

In keeping with its commitment to lawful work, the New Dawn group cooperated with leftist members of the Wafd whose goal was to radicalize their party. To that end, it supported the Wafdist Vanguard (al-Talia al-Wafdiyya) which was an organization of intellectual youth inside the Wafd. It arose after the close of World War II when Egyptian youth renewed their hope for national independence. Under the leadership of Dr. Muhammad Mandur and Dr. Aziz Fahmi, the organization attempted to move the center of the Wafd to the left by providing the party with a revolutionary social and nationalist program.[41]

Acting as a pressure group, the Wafdist Vanguard publicized the importance of understanding the national question in world terms and identified the economic bases of imperialism. Internationally, it looked favorably on the socialist powers and supported movements of national liberation. In Egypt it defended the rights of the workers and peasants by criticizing the excesses of capitalist exploitation and by exposing the abuses of rural landholding.[42]

Influenced by liberal and socialist thought, the Wafdist Vanguard revealed some communality with the Marxist forces which were simultaneously coming into their own in Egypt. It was especially as a result of the antidemocratic measures adopted by successive Prime Ministers Nuqrashi, Sidqi, and Abd al-Hadi, that the rapprochement between the Wafdist Vanguard and the Marxists occurred. In point of fact, the communist underground welcomed alliance between the two movements because anti-establishment activity, especially in the university, was fortified by the combination. In particular, members of the New Dawn worked with the Wafdist Vanguard through the Executive Committee of Students, in which the Wafdist left predominated, and also by contributing to the liberal Wafdist newspaper *Rabitat al-Shabab* (The League of Youth). That normally sectarian communists felt comfortable enough to write in Wafdist newspapers is a measure of their mutual integration.

In 1945 and 1946, the New Dawn group used the influential journal *al-Fajr al-Jadid* as a platform for the publication of its ideas. In its pages, the existing political leadership was criticized for its inability to improve the conditions of the popular classes and for its failure to achieve national independence. Capitalists, large landowners, high civil servants, and those writers and thinkers who supported them were considered representatives of a single class which neither supported democracy nor contributed to the economic well-being of the mass of the population.[43] The magazine called for raising the standard of living of workers and peasants, the introduction of labor legislation in agriculture, limiting land ownership, and the imposition of progressive taxation.[44]

Through sophisticated literary production, the group attracted the attention of the intellectual circles of Egypt. But its influence went beyond the narrow confines of intellectuals: it exerted its presence among workers as well. Its principal contacts were with the Workers' Committee for National Liberation (WCNL) which was formed in August 1945. It members, communists and left-wing trade unionists, numbered about eighty, but its influence was more widely spread among approximately four thousand textile workers from Shubra al-Khayma and Mahalla al-Kubra. The Committee called for Egypt's liberation from imperialism, the complete independence of the Nile Valley, the institution of democracy, and a series of improvements and benefits for workers.[45] Symbolizing the marriage between socialist thought and the working class, the WCNL represented a new point of view in Egypt.

In a bid for international recognition, the WCNL sent its representative Muhammad Yusuf al-Mudarrik, a member of the International Shopkeepers' Union, to Paris in September 1945 as one of the Egyptian delegates to the World Federation of Trade Unions' Conference. While he was unable to obtain the recognition of the Conference as the sole emissary of Egyptian trade unions, he nonetheless distributed the WCNL's own literature and brought back plans for developing the Egyptian labor movement.

On his return from Paris, Muhammad Yusuf al-Mudarrik, together with Mahmud al-Askari, formerly a weaver in a Shubra textile factory, Taha Saad Uthman, a leader of the mechanized textile workers' union, and Dr. Abd al-Karim Sukkari started publishing the newspaper *al-Damir* which they circulated widely in industrial areas. The newspaper contained reprints of articles from the Daily Worker and from French communist newspapers as well as articles about the economic and political situation in Egypt.

Until Sidqi's strike against his opposition in July 1946, the New Dawn group engaged strictly in legal activity. It was only after the July 11 episode when *al-Fajr al-Jadid*, *al-Damir*, and the Modern Culture Society were dissolved that Ahmad Sadiq Saad, Raymond Duwayk, Yusuf Darwish, and Ahmad Rushdi Salih decided to form a secret Marxist organization. They contacted friends who had established a deep-seated relationship with *al-Fajr al-Jadid* and *al-Damir* and set up meetings during which the four organizers presented their associates with the basis for an underground party; the rules, the political, organizational, popular and trade union postures. After an agreement was forged, the first name given the new party was the Popular Vanguard for Liberation (al-Talia al-Shaabiyya lil Taharrur).[46] A short time later it was changed to the Workers' Vanguard (Taliat al-Ummal) and subsequently to Popular Democracy (al-Dimuqratiyya al-Shaabiyya). Being very secretive, the name of the organization was not even announced. Hilmi Yassin, a member of the organization, recalled a funny story:

> In May 1948 when one of our comrades from Shubra went to the concentration camp, one of the officers said, "Come on Tisht."

Tisht is the name for the basin you wash your clothes in, but it also means a kind of insult as well. At the same time it stands for the initials T.Sh.T.— al-Talia al-Shaabiyya lil Taharrur. The imprisoned man did not know the name of the organization and he thought the officer was insulting him. One of our comrades had to tell him that this was the name of our party.[47]

At the base of the Popular Vanguard for Liberation were workers drawn largely from the textile factories of Shubra al-Khayma and Minya, the cotton mills of Alexandria, and the marine industries of Port Said.[48] Urban intellectuals were also recruited. Membership was open to those who approved of the party's program, submitted to its decisions, became active in one of its organizations, and paid regular monthly dues. The party functioned according to the principle of democratic centralism which meant that party leaders were elected, discussions were held on all levels of the organization, and strict party discipline was respected. Moreover, the decisions of the highest levels of the party were binding on lower levels of the organization. The basic organizational unit was the group or cell. Groups were organized in the workplace or in residences: in factories, workshops, stores, schools, companies, villages, or neighborhoods. Three members made up a group and there was no separation according to occupation, religion, or ethnic background.[49] Three to ten groups constituted a section, three to ten sections composed a branch. Area committees stood above branches, and party conferences were to be held every two years to determine the policies, tactics, rules, and program to be followed, as well as the make up of the central committee.[50]

The Popular Vanguard for Liberation set up a women's committee in order to politicize and organize women comrades. It proposed:

- to distribute internal propaganda within the party to fight reactionary ideology among the male comrades themselves with regard to women's role in the socialist cause
- to show interest in the struggle of women in factories and institutions
- to discuss the possibility of mobilizing comrades' wives and sisters
- to watch the behavior of men with sisters and wives
- to direct the female forces to work among women factory workers, housewives, and students
- to publicize the political and economic problems of women and housewives and to agitate about the rising cost of living.[51]

Despite its efforts, the party never really recruited working-class women because of its limited resources and the general political conservatism in Egyptian society.

When the Popular Vanguard was founded as an underground organization, it was both nationalist and trade unionist in orientation. The party hoped to participate in, and perhaps sometime direct, nationalist agitation in an effort to politicize a wide range of people. Its attempt to organize the working class and to create independent, radical trade unions, was a tactic it presumed could best serve the socialist cause and, in fact, it was to the workplace, and specifically to the factory, that its limited resources were directed.

The organization did not harbor visions of forming a vanguard communist party. Its membership numbered only in the hundreds and its impact on Egyptian politics was small. But through its political organization and commitment to journalism it was responsible for carrying forward important oppositional ideas and, in addition, it radicalized a number of trade union leaders through its consistent defense of workers' demands and rights.

The National Movement after World War II

Egypt in 1946 was a changed and changing country. A new consciousness was born tied directly to the disruptions in the international situation emerging out of World War II. Nationalist demands which had been current since the days of Saad Zaghlul resurfaced and were now infused with new expectations and possibilities. British evacuation from the Nile Valley became an urgent appeal supported by a broad cross section of the Egyptian populace. The three explosive weeks between February 9, and March 4, 1946, to be discussed below, were a product of this heightened consciousness.

After the termination of press censorship and the abolition of martial law in August of 1945, the clamor for independence began immediately. Since Egyptians played a supportive role during the war and suffered the consequences of economic and social disruption, they wanted to be rewarded by a British commitment to pull their troops off Egyptian and Sudanese soil. In the face of popular agitation, Prime Minister Nuqrashi, in December of 1945, called for fresh negotiations with the British in the hope of securing full Egyptian independence. Britain's equivocal reply in January of 1946 was negatively received in Egypt. The enmity it produced touched off the February 1946 demonstrations in Cairo, Alexandria, and the provinces. Jamal Ghali, a student leader, recalled those turbulent days at Cairo University:

> In September 1945, at the end of the summer holidays, students from different faculties in the university gathered at the Faculty of Medicine. Students from Law, Science, the Arts began discussing what should be done in 1946. It was the end of the war and we believed we should start the liberation movement for complete Egyptian independence. At these meetings there were three influences: the Wafd, the Muslim Brotherhood and the progressive movement which meant Iskra and the EMNL. We discussed liberation for Egypt and the Sudan and economic targets. . . . Later, during October, November and December a committee was formed which agitated among students in the university. Parallel to that, there was an effort to make a united trade union movement in Egypt. . . . In 1946, there was contact between this embryonic student organization . . . and this trade union movement. By January 1946 there was an upsurge of activity among students, student elections were held and delegates were selected to make contacts with the workers.[52]

The Executive Committee of Students of the University and High Institutes to which Jamal Ghali indirectly referred decided to call a massive demonstration on February 9 to protest the colonial occupation. On that day, students met by the thousands and moved from the university grounds in Giza, marching toward Abdin Palace. They chanted "Evacuation: No negotiations except after evacuation!" When they approached the Abbas Bridge, the students found it surrounded by police officers. A clash occurred and Salim Zaki Pasha, Commandant of the Cairo City Police, ordered the Abbas Bridge opened while students were crossing it.[53] This resulted in the deaths of over twenty students by drowning[54] and in eighty-four serious casualties.[55] Many considered this a premeditated assault on the students, since when Salim Zaki was asked on an earlier occasion how he might contend with an anti-British mob attack, he replied, "'that will stop them' . . . pointing to the broad waters of the Nile, 'its all I've got, anyway.'"[56]

As a result of the student deaths, demonstrations erupted in parts of Mansura, Zagazig, Aswan, Shabin al-Kom, Alexandria, and Cairo. Nuqrashi was forced to resign on February 15; he was succeeded by

Ismail Sidqi. There was increased hostility directed toward the King, the "street" was active not only in the cities but also in the towns of the provinces, and the growing participation of the working class was increasingly evident. The question was how to coordinate the diverse elements of the nationalist movement to demonstrate the national outrage at the Abbas Bridge incident and to protest the indignity of the continued occupation. The answer was found in the National Committee of Workers and Students (NCWS) which was born about a week after the confrontation between the students and the police. An unsigned communist tract gave the following reason for the establishment of the NCWS:

> That at the time the students saw . . . that they would not be able to go alone into the national struggle. It was the same with the workers who were struggling to gain their rights in their various districts, and also struggling for national demands. So the workers strove to join their struggle with that of the students, and the students to the workers. . . . Thus, a historical welding was brought about, and the Committee of Workers and Students was formed which led the nationalist struggle. . . .[57]

From every faculty at the university five students were elected to a general students' committee. From this committee fifteen or twenty students were selected to meet with a similar number of workers from the textile factories, the tram and transport unions, and the service unions, to form the NCWS.[58] The Committee established three central goals:

- to struggle for national independence and to combat the military occupation and economic, political, cultural, and colonial domination
- to eliminate the local agents of colonialism, i.e., feudalists and big financiers connected with foreign monopolies
- to unite all the anticolonialist nationalist forces, to support mass demonstrations and strikes, and to forge contacts with international anti-colonial and democratic movements.[59]

The NCWS saw itself as a broad front which embraced both the nationalist and class struggles and which included communists, Wafdists, democrats, workers, and students. The demonstrations and strikes it organized symbolized the activity of people on the streets but were not an expression of disciplined or mature political activism.[60] Though the very birth of the Committee reflects the radical social and political changes which followed World War II, the Committee was only of temporary importance. It was ultimately doomed to failure because it lacked both a stable organizational structure and anything approaching theoretical clarity. Thus, once the exuberance of February faded, it was an easy target for liquidation by the government. Sharif Hatata suggested that:

> The National Committee of Workers and Students was a very fluid body; that is why almost anyone who participated in the national movement in 1946 or 1947 can say that he was, at one time or another, a member. People were coming and going all the time. People used to drop out and others used to come and replace them. It wasn't a very circumscribed body so that sometimes people used to be members without being elected. People would just be there carrying out assignments or tasks within the Committee.

As to the role played by militant communists in the Committee, Hatata added:

> Those who were organized within the left-wing movement were probably the most conscious of the elements that existed. And probably many of the suggestions came from them because they saw things somewhat more clearly. They also had a sense of organization. But it wasn't meticulously planned or worked out in previous sessions within the organization. . . . It was much more irregular and chaotic. . . . There was an element of revolutionary instinct, a feel of what should be done. Also, what the communists did and what nobody had done before was to create the linkages between the economic struggle of the workers and the national movement and between the national movement and social change. The linkages were created by students, intellectuals and political thinkers who contacted the workers and started to organize them, to impart knowledge to them. But because of the youth of the left-wing movement, its capacity to encompass it and organize it and work in it systematically was still limited.[61]

There were members of Iskra, the EMNL, and the Wafdist Vanguard on the NCWS which allowed for wide communication and interchange between the political groups. For once, the sectarianism of the left was overcome by the force of events. What seems to have happened was that the national movement rose spontaneously as a result of prevailing conditions. The left-wing movement, rather than inspiring it, tried desperately to build into it and in some way direct it. The Committee, with the help of the left, did have some political vision, but it lacked the organizational force and political sophistication which could have sustained it in the face of governmental repression.

Two of the important events the Committee did stage were the demonstration and general strike of February 21, 1946, and the March 4 day of mourning. February 21 was to be celebrated as a day of national unity and complete independence from the imperialist yoke, with huge demonstrations in Cairo, Alexandria, and other cities. It was meant as a gesture of defiance aimed at Ismail Sidqi's dictatorial government. On that day, communications workers stopped their work and gathered together in Giza, Shubra al-Khayma, and Abbasiyya, and began moving in large demonstrations toward downtown Cairo. Workers from the railway union and from the workshops of Abu Zaabal, from the pharmaceutical and woodworking industries, from textile factories and commercial shops from Helwan, Imbaba, and Ghamra started marching toward Cairo. Students from the university, from al-Azhar, and from lower schools proceeded first to Midan al-Opera then to Midan al-Ismailiyya.[62] Demonstrators were chanting, "No colonialism, no bondage; evacuation or sacrifice."[63]

From most accounts, the demonstration was peaceful until the protesters were incited by the behavior of British military personnel. Although previously instructed by their superiors to stay out of the area on the day of the demonstration, several military cars came through the crowds, possibly injuring some of the protesters.[64] The armored cars seemed a gratuitous affront to the national cause and their presence evidently induced the crowd to attack the British. After a struggle broke out between the two sides, more violence and destruction occurred as demonstrators attacked foreign shops, clubs, and the British military camp. At the end of the day there were twenty-three dead and one hundred and twenty-one wounded.[65] The victims were given martyrs' funerals and the collective anger was exacerbated.[66] Tensions ran high and demonstrations spread to Giza, Shubra al-Khayma, Bab al-Sharqiyya, Misr al-Jadida, Abbasiyya, Helwan, Port Said, Ismailiyya, Zagazig, Mansura, Zifta, Mahalla al-Kubra, and Tanta.

Following the confrontation, the NCWS met and passed a number of resolutions among which was the establishment of a day of mourning on March 4 in remembrance of those people who fell on February 21. Members of the committee went to the government and asked for the cooperation of the army, police, and civil servants. Sidqi Pasha, who doubted whether the crowd could be controlled, tried to dissuade the Committee from its intention to demonstrate on March 4. He alleged that the British Ambassador had warned him that the British armed forces were prepared to fire on the demonstrators. The Committee was not impressed and attested to the determination of the people to observe the day of mourning. Thus, when March 4 came, newspapers were not printed, coffee shops, stores, and factories were closed down, schools and universities were silent. The Egyptian people were responding to the new nationalist leadership. Cairo passed the day quietly, but in Alexandria, a clash between the demonstrators and the police left 28 dead and 342 wounded.[67]

During the rising tide of nationalist sentiment from February through July 1946, the Egyptian people who participated in the demonstrations and strikes of the period believed they were defending their legitimate rights. They took for granted the notion that they represented a wide body of public opinion. Their main objective was the evacuation of the British from the Nile Valley. What finally triggered them into action was their frustration and impatience with the traditional pattern of Anglo-Egyptian negotiations. With the war over, people expected the beginning of a new era, one which would bring with it national dignity and prosperity. This was to be heralded in by the commitment of the British to withdraw their occupation forces. Instead, British hesitation generated growing popular resentment. The Egyptian authorities themselves lost the confidence and trust of the populace who were unable to identify with any of the traditional political parties which were theoretically organized to represent their interests.

The form of protest embraced by the Egyptian crowd was that of the demonstration. Direct action was not new to the Egyptian people; demonstrations, as a model of political protest, were part of the Egyptian nationalist heritage. The street had in the past, and probably would in the future, rise up given the right circumstances and leadership. Historically, not all Egyptian protests have been controllable. Yet, a notable feature of the stormy days of February and March was the restraint and discipline of the demonstrators.[68]

When on March 8, the British announced their intention to

evacuate the Cairo, Alexandria, and Delta zones and set up military camp only in the region of the Suez Canal, the NCWS, with the rest of the left, took this proclamation as their victory over the forces of imperialism. Whether this sentiment reflected reality is still unclear. Nevertheless, the February and March events pointed at once to the instability of the Sidqi regime, the precariousness of the British occupation, and the growing strength of the Egyptian leftwing opposition when tied to a mass movement. Still, in early 1946, the NCWS was very fragile; consequently, the government was able to crush the Committee easily after the enthusiasm of the moment had subsided.

Sidqi himself was aware of his uncertain position and sensitive to British dissatisfaction with his seeming lack of control. In retaliation against the unity of the people around the NCWS, Sidqi tightened the reins. He moved against the opposition on July 11, 1946, with the arrest of hundreds of journalists, intellectuals, political and labor leaders, students and professionals, on sometimes trumped up charges of communist affiliation. In addition, he ordered the dissolution of eleven political, cultural, and labor organizations and closed down leftwing and Wafdist journals.

Although over two hundred people were initially apprehended by the police in what was considered the government's biggest anti-communist court case ever, only sixty-nine were finally accused and only twenty were charged with criminal behavior.[69] Those accused included, according to the transcript of the court case itself: one doctor, eight employees of banks, companies or the government, twenty-one university students, four secondary school teachers, four university teachers, eighteen journalists, five lawyers, two al-Azhar students or graduates, five workers. Seven of the accused were women.[70] Those charged lived in Cairo, Alexandria, Giza, Port Said, and Suez. Among those arrested were some with affiliations to the communist underground. However, there was never a reference to the clandestine political movement during the court proceedings. This suggests that the authorities were fundamentally uninformed about the membership and activities of the Marxist groups. That they happened to strike communists along with liberals, democrats, and the opposition in general, was a simple function of the political leaning of those who participated in and led the demonstrations. The government's intention seems to have been to silence the dissent and political activity of any group left of liberal center.

The Sidqi regime closed down organizations whose militant activities reflected leftist tendencies. Among them were:

The House of Scientific Research
The Committee to Spread Modern Culture
The Union of University Graduates
The Popular University
The Twentieth Century Publishing House
The League of Women Graduates from the University and Higher
    Institutes
The Center for Popular Culture

In addition, eight opposition newspapers were banned:

al-Wafd al-Misri	central Wafdist organ
al-Bath	Wafdist daily
al-Damir	radical trade union paper
Umdurman	radical Sudanese magazine
al-Talia	Union of University Graduates magazine
al-Fajr al-Jadid	radical cultural weekly
al-Yara and *al-Jabha*	two trade union weeklies

Lastly, three bookstores were closed, among which was al-Midan Bookstore owned by Henri Curiel.

In order to publicize the antidemocratic tactics of Sidqi, a report was sent from Egypt to the International League for the Defense of Human Rights. It described Sidqi's crusade against the opposition as follows:

It started at midnight (July 10, 1946). Sidqi used hundreds of armed policemen, secret agents and members of the prosecution. It lasted until 9:00 a.m. on the following day. Over 250 flats were literally turned upside and down. Every paper, every book was examined. . . .

Bedrooms were forced open and wives and sisters undressed, were terrorized with armed policemen pointing guns at the bed. . . .

A hundred and seventy-two people were arrested and put in prison for days on end without being interrogated although the law explicitly specifies that no one should be kept more than twenty-four hours without being questioned. . . .

The newspapers were forbidden, and still are so, to write anything about the case, secrecy being considered as necessary. Even the lawyers were prevented from attending the investigation or knowing anything about the charges. . . .

A conclusive proof of the unsoundness of the whole fabricated charge was the release of all the accused after one to three months being kept in jail, some on bail and many others without bail. Had there been the least evidence, they would have been kept in prison.[71]

It was not surprising that Sidqi was determined to crush the democratic movement. Known in the country as the "strongman" of Egypt, his antidemocratic tendencies were well established. Once before, in 1930, when Egypt was in the midst of economic and political crisis, Sidqi was appointed Prime Minister. To inaugurate his regime, he dissolved Parliament and abolished the Constitution. What followed were three years of unbridled dictatorship which are remembered by the people as one of the harshest episodes in modern Egyptian history. A monopolist with sizable interests in the textile and fruit industries, he served as President of the Egyptian Federation of Industries, a powerful group of capitalists who represented both Egyptian and foreign interests. His distaste for socialism, communism, or indeed any form of liberalism, cannot be questioned. After the turbulent days of February and March 1946, Sidqi pretended to have unearthed a communist plot to overthrow the existing regime and hence ordered the mass arrests of July. Sidqi's use of the word communist was, of course, quite loose, applying it as he did to all those of a liberal or radical nature who tended to criticize or wanted to alter the Egyptian status quo.

Following Sidqi's campaign of arrests, a new law was promulgated and added to Article 98 in Chapter II of the Penal Code of 1937. This chapter dealt with crimes against the internal security of the state. The new sections provided punishment for the promoters of revolutionary societies whose aims included the subordination of one social class to another, the overthrow of a social class, or the destruction of the fundamental social or economic principles of the state. Additional sections provided for the punishment of agitators who tried to change the basic principles of the Constitution and forbade the formation, without governmental permission, of organizations with an international character. This was a new weapon devised by Sidqi to be used against all advocates of reform who could in the future be branded with the label of subversive communist.

Sidqi took advantage of the calm prevailing in Egypt after his opposition was arrested and flew to London to resume withdrawal negotiations with British Foreign Secretary Bevin. The agreement reached stipulated that the British would withdraw from Cairo, Alexandria, and the Delta, as previously announced, by March 1947, and from all of Egypt by September 1949. A military defense pact was agreed upon which stipulated that in the event that either Egypt or England was involved in a war with countries adjacent to Egypt, both governments would take measures until the Security Council acted. Finally, Sudan was to remain under Egyptian rule until self-government was achieved. Still less than a grant of full independence for Egypt, the agreement met with opposition from Egyptians. Likewise, it faced criticism in England because the pro-Sudanese lobby thought it had given too much away to Egypt. Failure to secure an agreement forced Sidqi to resign on December 8, 1946. Nuqrashi, his successor, took Egypt's case before the Security Council of the United Nations in 1947 to appease nationalist feelings in the country and to defend Egypt's interests. His voice was barely heard and the Council recommended a resumption of negotiations to the extreme disappointment of Egyptian society. It was this sort of ineffectual performance that made it increasingly clear that the traditional parties were incapable of solving the national question.

4

Unification and Division in the
Communist Movement, 1947–1954

As THE NATIONALIST MOVEMENT in Egypt was flaring, the lack of unity among revolutionary leftist organizations was exposed as a fundamental problem. Prior to the nationalist surge, the sectarian squabbling among the predominantly upper class and semi-foreign intellectuals who made up the communist movement was of largely academic interest. Once large numbers of people became politicized around the cause of nationalism, however, the division of the revolutionary left had enormous practical implications. Almost against their will, the revolutionary leaders had to submerge their ideological and personal differences if they were—through unity—to play a significant role in shaping the course of the nationalist struggle.

At the end of May 1947, the leaderships of the EMNL and Iskra joined forces.[1] A new organization, the Democratic Movement for National Liberation (DMNL) was formed, and called Hadeto. [The name Hadeto is an acronym and stands for al-Haraka al-Dimuqratiyya lil Taharrur al-Watani.] This became the largest, most important, and most enduring communist organization in Egypt during the latter 1940s and 1950s and as such deserves special comment.

The Democratic Movement for National Liberation

In May 1947 there were approximately 1,700 communists organized in the DMNL, with about 800 from the EMNL and the remaining from Iskra and the smaller People's Liberation movement.[2] The DMNL organized itself on a functional basis, typically establishing cells, branches, and sections.[3] Sections were designed so that similar types of people with presumably shared experiences and already established associations, such as groups of Jews, Azharites, workers, or soldiers, would meet together. (See Figure 2.) This form of organization was Curiel's creation and a carry-over from the EMNL. Curiel believed that the sections provided the party a valuable service by allowing supporters to accommodate themselves to the movement in the most familiar environment.[4] Above the sections stood the secretariat which executed the many decisions and directives of the central committee. The core of the movement, the central committee, was responsible for the policies, the organizational forms, the finances, and the cultural activities.

The DMNL was financed exclusively from subscriptions and contributions imposed upon party members. In addition, membership required cadres to undertake a Marxist-Leninist education, attend meetings regularly, and send reports about their neighborhood and work experiences to their superiors. They were required to be absolutely secret about their own responsibilities and every aspect of the party.[5] However, among the major weaknesses of the DMNL was the vulnerability of its security system and the profound inability to discipline members and provide them adequate protection from the authorities.

By the latter 1940s the political police had become increasingly more sophisticated in its methods to combat communism. With extensive resources committed to punishing the opposition, many communists were arrested and imprisoned. Actually, the police found it relatively easy to track down numbers of communists, mainly because of the very limited precautions taken by the leftists themselves. Instead of shunning the company of fellow communists, members openly socialized with each other. Once the police learned the whereabouts of a single party member, the status of other cadres was compromised as well.

Consider the experience of Muhammad Fuad Munir and Muhammad Shatta, two DMNL members who were arrested in March 1952 for their affiliation with the organization.[6] After the coup d'etat of July 1952, a decision was taken to release all but fourteen political prisoners from jail. Though Muhammad Fuad Munir and Muhammad Shatta were among those who remained detained, they managed to escape from Qasr al-Ayni Hospital where as prisoners they were receiving medical attention. With the help of a "foreign" woman who drove the getaway car, Shatta and Munir proceeded to the house of their comrade Sharif Hatata.

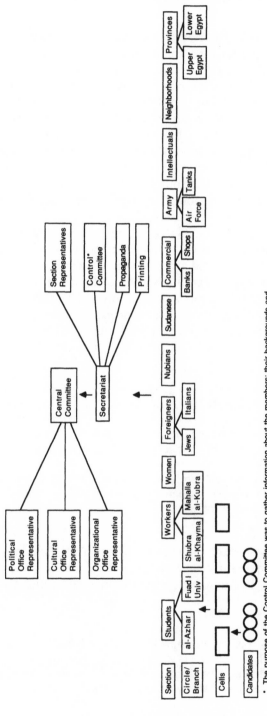

Figure 2

A Sectional View of the Structure of the Democratic Movement for National Liberation

* The purpose of the Control Committee was to gather information about the members: their backgrounds and their past and present activities. In essence, it was formed to ensure that no members were police agents.

Hatata himself was hardly a safe contact: he had been under surveillance by the authorities, spent time in jail for communist activities, and was still an active member of the DMNL. The very choice of his house as a hideout reflected a breakdown in party security: appropriate behavior would have led them to find sanctuary in a more concealed place. After remaining in Hatata's house for several days, they were visited by Fuad Habashi, another DMNL member, who informed the hideaways that their whereabouts had been discovered, information which forced them to leave Hatata's premises. But instead of finding a neutral place to keep out of sight, they moved to Habashi's flat in Shubra. All four were now living in the same location, sitting ducks for the police, and were arrested.

Perhaps surprisingly, the relatively unprotected security system did not prevent the organization from carrying out significant propaganda efforts. In fact, it issued a volume of publications and leaflets which can be seen both as a tribute to the resilience of the organization and as a sign of the openness of the times. The DMNL considered the printing of a sophisticated legal newspaper a very important priority and it worked from the very beginning to achieve the goal of journalistic competence. In an early tract the party stated:

> The paper must certainly play a part in everything touching the life of the masses, that is, it must become a pulpit for expressing the pains and hopes of the peasants, students, small government employees and women, and the way for exposing every persecution and oppression wherever such persecution and oppression shall appear.
>
> In this way we can firmly bind the paper to the life of the masses in their daily struggle and can attract a large section of them to the political struggle.[7]

Because a newspaper had the potential of raising the level of consciousness of members and of attracting sympathizers to the radical cause, it needed to be interesting, relevant and accessible. A DMNL memo noted:

> When we write, our writing must not be dry and theoretical, unconnected with those subjects which are of interest to people – if there is a lot of talk about Zionism, then we bring out a theoretical study of it. And instead of writing generally about art we must

analyze the starting point of any film or we must analyze a certain story to discover the progressive or reactionary elements in it. If we write an Egyptian short story it must be connected with the lives of the masses and possess an element of instruction.

The more news that comes from the country(side) and the factories and schools and poor quarters . . . the more does our link with the masses in our daily struggle increase and the more do our possibilities for directing these masses increase.[8]

Operating under the assumption that meaningful publications contributed directly to a live and active organization, the party published internal bulletins as well as newspapers for open consumption. The DMNL's clandestine party papers included *al-Qaida* (The Base), and *al-Kifah* (The Struggle), *al-Talia* (The Vanguard), and *Saut al-Fallahin* (The Voice of the Peasants).[9] These publications were produced secretly, being either typewritten or handwritten, duplicated, and distributed only to members of the organization. Although guidance and directives on policy were transmitted by the central committee downward, all members were encouraged to contribute articles on their particular areas of work and any problems they encountered as party members.

The main channels of legal propaganda geared to a wider audience included first *al-Jamahir* (The Masses) and later *al-Malayin* (The Millions) and *al-Wajib* (The Duty). *Al-Jamahir* had an estimated paid circulation in 1948 of 8000 but since many of the unsold copies were distributed free in working class districts, it may have had a considerably wider readership than its circulation figures would suggest.[10]

The organization also published the radical newspaper The Voice of the Students as an aid in educating and politicizing students and influencing university politics. The paper was linked with the Egyptian League for Students, which was a DMNL front. Although the party had no exclusive publication geared specifically to the community of al-Azhar, it set recruitment there as an important priority and published pamphlets identifying its position. One handout remarked:

Men of religion in this country have always played an important part against imperialism — French, Turkish, English. At present Zahra [code name for al-Azhar] is standing at the crossroads between the people and the bourgeoisie. The importance of Zahra is as follows: they are the religious body which assists reaction; their men represent the working classes; they enjoy spiritual con-

fidence among the people; their roots go deep among many classes
of Egyptians—teachers, preachers, Imams, etc.

As they are so important we must win them away from reaction and the Palace.

Our aims. To make the Azharites join in the national struggle with us. We must not allow the Azharites to be a toy in the
hands of reaction.[11]

In order to produce its newspapers, pamphlets, and bulletins,
which were written in Arabic, English, and French, and circulated
among the members, the organization set up a special propaganda unit.
Under its control were a secret press, typewriters, and a number of
stenciling machines. Depending on the type of manuscript involved,
publications were either handwritten, typewritten and duplicated, or
printed. They were significant in helping to spread party ideas among
key groups in Egyptian society: in particular among workers, students,
military men, peasants, and nationalists.

Despite the composition of the DMNL's leadership, which was
disproportionately middle or upper class and intellectual, recruiting
members from the more dispossessed groups in society and address-
ing their daily economic and nationalist struggles were primary aims.
Workers were considered a central group in the DMNL and an organ,
Kifah al-Ummal (The Workers' Struggle), was dedicated to them. Devoted almost entirely to labor and trade union issues, it was distributed in industrial areas by members of the party. Through it, the
DMNL had some success in the textile workers' unions, the trans-
portation union, among wire and wireless communications workers,
hotel workers, sea workers, tobacco workers, and military men.[12] Although labor leaders, whose growing sophistication predisposed them
to radical solutions to labor problems, were the first to become involved, some common workers also joined in.

Muhammad Gad might be considered typical of the kind of rank
and file worker who was recruited by the party. Born in the humble
Muski section of Cairo in 1910, he left school at the primary level
and, like his father, became a carpenter. As a young boy during the
1920s he was attentive to the conflicts between Saad Zaghlul, King
Fuad and the British, participated in the Wafdist-organized demonstrations, and became active in the nationalist movement. Like those
of his generation, he hoped for the establishment of complete independence at the close of World War II and with the "enthusiasm of
youth" he pressed for change.

In the later years of the war, Gad began frequenting the cafe Issayivitch in downtown Cairo which became known as a meeting place for leftists, democrats, and avant-garde artists. There Gad met Henri Curiel and others from the communist movement. In a number of sessions spanning months, he sat among a group of leftists who discussed the nationalist movement, Egyptian economic development, the class structure of the country, and the international situation. At Issayivitch, he acquired something of a political education. He joined the EMNL and later the DMNL where he remained during the length of his underground career.

Through Gad and other trade unionists, the DMNL became involved in direct and confrontational activity in the workplace. The party encouraged labor unrest by engaging the most politically active union members. Specifically, the DMNL directed attention to the low wages, poor working conditions, and repressive labor legislation to which workers were subjected. While it would be a gross exaggeration to attribute all the work stoppages between 1945 and 1952 to the communists, they did contribute strongly to the labor activism of the period.

The Misr Spinning and Weaving Company in Mahalla al-Kubra, which was the largest and most modern textile factory in Egypt, provides a good example of the DMNL's role in urging increased worker militancy in this period. The Misr Company, which was an Egyptian concern, was linked with the Bradford Dyers Association. Labor relations between the management and the workers were less than harmonious. In late August 1947, the company's assistant factory director decided that twelve workers who had been openly carrying on subversive agitation among the workers should be separated from the group and transferred to other sections of the factory. These workers refused to accept the transfer and were dismissed. They were told that their severance pay, as provided by the Labor Code, would be paid to them in ten days, on September 2. From the time of their discharge until September 2, these twelve workers continued their political activities among workers during off-hours in the town of Mahalla al-Kubra. Their main contention was that the company had lately received new labor-saving machinery and was preparing to dismiss some 12,000 workers.

In early September the dismissed workers went to the factory to collect their termination indemnities and noticed the company had posted new internal working regulations. These regulations provided for disciplinary action, fines, and in some cases dismissal in the event of noncompliance. The dismissed workers understood these measures as proof of their allegations that the company was preparing to dismiss large numbers of workers.

It did not take long before rumors of impending dismissals spread throughout the factory convincing workers to set down their tools and begin to demonstrate. Fearing destruction of company property, the employer instituted a lock-out at the hour when the second shift was to take over. Most of the nine thousand second-shift workers, together with other workers from the town of Mahalla, demonstrated during the afternoon and into the night. The climax occurred when a group of workers looted the clinic and a warehouse and advanced toward the residence of the assistant director of the factory. By this time, the police had been reinforced by several hundred officers from Tanta, and force was used to break up the demonstrations. One worker was killed and a number of others were injured.

On the morning of September 3, another large demonstration took place; tempers became quite heated and some two thousand workers began breaking windows in Mahalla. The local police intervened and after a battle three workers were killed. When the police ranks were later strengthened by soldiers from Cairo, the situation became quieter and the disorder ceased. In total about seventy workers were arrested. It was not until one week later that the factory reopened and work returned to its regular pace.

The strike was massively supported despite the fact that the textile workers' union, as a body, was a company union and had little independence of action. One indication of this was that the union's officers were direct company appointees. It is, therefore, not surprising that during the disturbances many of the workers called for the abolition of the union and frequently shouted out, "Down with the yellow union."

Few denied that the strike was stamped with a communist mark. The DMNL had been issuing a series of inflammatory leaflets during the previous month. Its members were active in the area and its slogans were continually being repeated. During the dispute the DMNL dispatched a proclamation to textile workers in Shubra al-Khayma asking them to support the workers in Mahalla "in their brave struggle." In fact, on September 5, some 17,000 textile workers in Shubra went on strike for one day in sympathy with their union brethren.

The Mahalla dispute effectively ended to the company's advantage, however, when work was resumed at the old rates of pay and under the newly imposed prestrike conditions. The only concession made by the company was the granting of five days' wages disguised as a bonus for the Bairam holiday and an agreement to work alternate Sundays for two months to help the men make up some of their lost pay.[13] The strikers had been defeated.

It is unclear what the intentions of the strike leaders were. If they endeavored to win important concessions from the Misr Company, they failed, but if they hoped to sow labor unrest they succeeded at least temporarily: the turmoil in Mahalla was followed by strikes by the textile workers in Alexandria, oil workers in Suez, telegraphists, and teachers. Moreover, during the following year another wave of strikes commenced as nurses, police officers, gas workers, and other textile workers protested their working conditions. Communist literature was found among some of the strikers but whether labor's defiance was inspired by the revolutionary left or merely exacerbated by it is uncertain.

Like its connection with workers, the DMNL's links with the military stretched back to the days of the EMNL. The organization's recruitment drives within the air force, the cavalry, the artillery, and among engineers, civilian technicians, and maintenance workers employed by the military were stamped with some success. In fact, a special section designed to guarantee optimum secrecy was set up in the party (a departure from the typically lax security regulations) exclusively for the military cadres. It was so effective that even fellow members of the organization were unaware of its existence. Ahmad Hamrush, one of those responsible for the military section in the DMNL, stated:

> Security was very important. If you didn't have security you would have given yourself easily to the police. I was very keen, then, that the members were not known outside our group. . . . We put security as number one because we were in the army and it was very difficult to be a communist in the army. However, it was possible for communists to work inside the army because the army was organized and disciplined. There were no leaks. People followed instructions. Meet at this place at this time and it was done. Read or don't read and it was done. This helped us very much.[14]

Ahmad Hamrush was an important recruit to the communist movement. Born in 1921 in Beni Suif, his family had predominantly agricultural roots. His father, who died when Ahmad was two years

old, became a judge in the religious courts. Hamrush was sent to
Cairo for his education and upon completion of secondary school, he
entered the Military College from which he graduated in 1948. Although Hamrush vacillated between joining Misr al-Fatat and the
Wafd as a secondary school student, by 1945 he made a firm decision to join the Marxist movement. His contribution to the DMNL's
military section was significant in that he offered a simple program
to military cadre which focused on national liberation from the British, the debilitating problem of poverty, and the scandalous behavior
of King Faruq.

Through the distribution and utilization of the "Green Books"—
the Marxist classics which members of the EMNL translated—the
educational, political, and cultural level of the military cadres was
raised. The DMNL organized officers, noncommissioned officers, and
only very rarely soldiers. Viewing the military as just one of a number of popular groups in society which could be subsumed under the
leadership of the party, the DMNL never perceived the military as
a potential vanguard of the revolution; nor, however, did the DMNL
develop a coherent revolutionary strategy of its own. Hamrush admitted:

> We just planned to organize ourselves, to strengthen ourselves,
> to distribute leaflets, to concentrate our opposition against the
> regime. But we never planned a way to put out this regime.[15]

The Free Officers, of course, were better prepared.

The DMNL inherited not only the connections which the EMNL
made in the military, but also the initiatives it began in the countryside.[16] In 1947 or 1948, the DMNL began directing appreciable energies toward the rural areas with the intention of solidifying the earlier contacts. Peasants were either recruited into the organization by
communist students returning to their villages during holidays or
sometimes by workers who belonged to peasant families.[17] Interest
in the radical cause was shown by very limited groups of poor peasants, agricultural laborers, and very small landowners.[18] Professional
revolutionaries who lived in the countryside, and used it as a place
of retreat and security from the police, managed the activity. The issues raised by the communists were generally related to land: land
reform, land tenure, peasant relationships with their landlords, and
the distribution of harvests. Party members advised peasants about

the possibilities of coordinating their farming procedures and collectivizing their agricultural efforts. Similarly, the problems of health, social services, and education were also brought to the fore.

In the countryside there was a committee of about nine professional revolutionaries whose responsibility it was to supervise the work among peasants and to serve as a link between the provinces and the organization's center in Cairo. The DMNL's cadres at work in Dakhaliyya, Sharqiyya, Zagazig, Minufiyya, Damanhur, Tanta, and Mansura in Lower Egypt or Asyut, Giza, or Beni Suif in Upper Egypt did not concentrate on organizing peasants in order to carry out underground activity. (See Figure 3.) Rather, the main goal was generally to raise the political struggle in the countryside and, specifically, to convince peasants of the need for cooperative farming as a way of defending their own rights.

The politicization and education of peasants was carried out in two ways. First, a cadres school was set up in the provinces and the most active sympathizers were brought together for periods of ten days. During these sessions the tenets of Marxism were discussed along with such topics as the significance of the Chinese Revolution and the historical struggles of the Egyptian peasant movement. The second method was through the party's newspapers *al-Jamahir* and *al-Malayin* but especially through *Saut al-Fallahin* (The Voice of the Peasants). The Voice of the Peasants was a semilegal publication, first begun in 1948, closed down sometime later, and reopened in 1953.[19] An editorial committee of five professionals decided what to publish and, in fact, authored many of the articles. Published nearly every month, it was printed on a stenciling machine and distributed in the provinces.

In addition to the information about land and agriculture, The Voice of the Peasants also published articles on international conferences dealing with agricultural labor; passed on village news; made criticisms of the military regime; provided reports on political prisoners, the national movement, and the Egyptian political scene generally.[20] The newspaper was published for political purposes: to give directives, to raise the consciousness of the readership, to exchange information between provinces. There was also, to be sure, an educational interest, and the paper contained descriptive articles explaining the importance of class, class struggle, agrarian reform, etc. An attempt was made to make the paper readable and informative and there was an effort to publish at least one article of a general nature focusing attention on the relationship between peasants and the wider

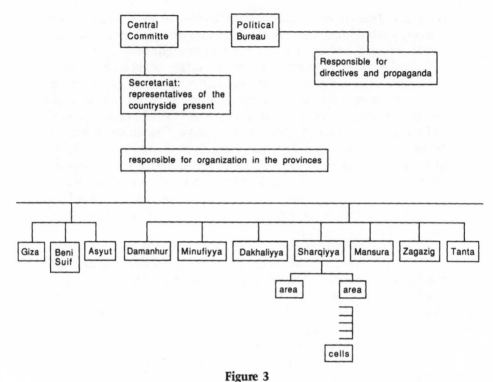

Figure 3
The Organizational Form of the
Democratic Movement for National Liberation

political situation. Sharif Hatata who was on the editorial staff commented:

> We were always very excited about what we did. We always felt it was tremendous. I think at the time, though, we probably exaggerated it. We didn't have a real assessment of what our actual strength was. Nevertheless, I think The Voice of the Peasants did play a relatively important role during that period. It came at a time when it was needed and contained things that were needed.[21]

Since most of the sympathetic peasants had a slightly higher level of political sophistication and education than the average *fal-*

lah, they could usually read and write. If there were illiterate peasants who were interested, the paper would be read to them by their
literate brethren in reading circles organized by the DMNL.[22]

From 1953 *Saut al-Fallahin* was published in the Delta region
in Tanta. Its size varied from six to seven pages depending on the circumstances and the difficulties of printing. Consistent with the time,
it was primarily concerned with the application of the agrarian reform laws which had been promulgated by the Revolutionary Command Council in September 1952. From that date there were heated
disputes between peasants and landlords centering on how the agrarian reform law should be implemented and about the need for agricultural trade unions, peasant cooperatives, and the fixing of rent.

The fact that the DMNL established a special section for the
countryside, sent its professional revolutionaries there to organize,
and instructed a particular editorial board to publish a special peasants' newspaper, demonstrated that work among peasants was a high
priority. Hatata maintained that:

> There was a vague attempt to shift the emphasis from the cities
> to the rural areas but there was always a greater attraction to the
> cities, being that we were urban people. Also, the center of the
> organization was in the city. If we were in the periphery we might
> be doing important work, but we were not in the center. One had
> to be a little pioneering to work in the rural areas—a bit selfless
> and, in fact, there were plenty of people like that.[23]

Michel Kamil, for example, was a professional revolutionary in the
early 1950s, who was given the difficult task of organizing in al-Said,
Upper Egypt. Though the greater part of the organization's work was
centralized in the big cities and industrial towns, he managed to bring
the DMNL's message to more inaccessible places such as Nag Hamadi
and Qina.

Although the DMNL had contacts in tens of villages by the early
1950s, the efforts of its organizers to radicalize peasants and to establish networks of oppositional strength were hampered by the progressive breakdown of the party's system of security in the provincial areas.
Especially after factionalism became rife and defections from the
DMNL increased from 1948 onward, the security in the countryside,
like that in the cities, began to disintegrate. The record of a political
court case based in Mansura in 1949 provides a glimpse of the organization's precarious security system in rural Egypt.

In 1948, Mahir Qandil, a ranking member of the party in Mansura, recruited his former school mate Saad into the party, exclusively on the basis of a past personal relationship. Before their reunion in 1948, Qandil had not seen Saad since 1941 and consequently knew little about his friend's interests, activities, and recent history. On the basis of several discussions with him, it appeared that Saad was enthusiastic about the radical cause. He was then admitted to the DMNL and was rapidly promoted within it.

At the time of Saad's quick advancement, around the outbreak of the Palestine War, communists were being arrested in large numbers across the country. As a result, the leadership was often incarcerated, leaving the management of the party to more inexperienced members like Mahir Qandil. In the case of the Mansura section of the DMNL, the party was seriously compromised; it was later revealed that Saad was a police agent who agreed to join the party in order to learn about its activities and report the information gathered to the authorities. Before quitting his job as infiltrator, Saad acquired enough detailed and damaging material to put many of Mansura's communists behind bars.

Saad's task was made easy by lapses of security committed by party members themselves. On a particular day, for example, Saad met a "comrade" whose party name was Sami at the latter's place of work. Sami invited Saad to his house where, upon entering, Saad noticed a door plaque on which Sami's real name was engraved. In one day, then, Saad learned Sami's workplace, home address, and real name.[24] At Sami's house two other members were introduced to Saad and a cell meeing was held. The issues discussed were, of course, conveyed to the police. Shortly after, word was circulated that the authorities were aware of the group's existence. A decision was taken to move all documents to Saad's house for safe keeping and from that time forward all materials were controlled by police officials.

As a member of the organization, Saad was asked to establish a connection with a peasant committee in Tanta. This gave the police an opportunity to uncover valuable information about party strength in the countryside. After agreeing to undertake the task, Saad made the necessary contacts through a secondary school student in his own cell and a student in Tanta. Through his Tanta intermediary, he was introduced to five peasants active in propagandizing communist ideas in the area.[25] He was informed about four communist cells in Tanta and their political activities.

During his discussions with the police, Saad explained the

DMNL's goals and philosophy as he was taught them: that by first creating a popular democratic movement as a step toward reaching socialism, communism could later be realized, and that by building a popular front of workers, peasants, and the petty bourgeoisie, the occupation forces would be evicted.[26] The informer's extensive information alerted the police to leftist ideology and activity in the countryside, and as a consequence, forced the DMNL to temper its political activity in the provinces. The experience of Mahir Qandil and Saad was not, however, an anomaly. The errors committed recurred again and again, crippling the effectiveness of the movement.

As an underground organization, the DMNL focused primarily on clandestine activity. However, the DMNL also found it advantageous to participate in open and legal political work as a way of establishing ties to other nationalist groups and widening the radical alliance. Between 1950 and 1952, when the Wafd was returned to power and a semblance of democratic life resumed, the DMNL concentrated on legal work. One of its important front groups, the Preparatory Committee to Found a General Trade Union, was established in the summer of 1951. With a working group which included representatives of 104 small unions, it boasted a membership of seventy thousand workers. Its goal was to help unify the trade union movement on a national scale. To this end it published the trade union newspaper *al-Wajib* as its organ. Despite its energetic activity, the Committee did not witness any major changes in labor legislation before 1952. However, after the Free Officers assumed power and recognized the right of workers to organize nationally, the DMNL believed its efforts netted significant labor results.[27]

Another arena of open activity for the DMNL was the Movement of Peace Supporters (Harakat Ansar al-Salam), which was formed in 1950 as the Egyptian branch of the World Peace Council. It gathered together individuals from the Wafd, the Muslim Brotherhood, the communist organizations, and Hizb al-Watani, and it attracted artists, actors, painters, writers, women, liberals, nationalists, and workers. Though not comprising a majority, the DMNL's members constituted an important and active minority. In keeping with its own experience of colonialism, the Egyptian group linked the cause of peace to national liberation.[28]

In an appeal to all Egyptians, the Peace Movement announced:

> Egypt is concerned about peace in the whole world so that Britain's excuse for occupying her territories, assaulting her indepen-

dence, dragging her sons to slaughter, destroying her economy and stealing hundreds of millions of her funds shall be nullified.[29]

Despite heavy censorship, the group published its message in the newspaper *al-Misri*. Inge Aflatun, one of its members, recalled how this was accomplished.

> We submitted the announcement to the editor of the paper after 3:00 in the afternoon which was the time the censor went home. Also, the editor was a friend of the Committee. This episode caused a reaction. The King said the paper must be confiscated. The government made a legal case out of it and the members of the Committee had to go before the prosecutor. We went before him and said, "Yes, we are guilty. We want peace." They could not make any arrests and so the case was dropped. It was a good beginning with a lot of publicity.[30]

Despite the repeated accusation that the peace committee was a communist front, it managed to attract a varied group of people holding different political views.[31] Since it was not a political party wed to any particular political ideology, its organ *al-Katib* (The Scribe) opened its columns to the left-Wafd, to the Muslim Brotherhood, and to the communists. Notwithstanding differences in party affiliation, the columnists shared some common beliefs, most notably that the British must evacuate Egypt and that the United States posed the principal threat to world peace.

With the burning of Cairo in January 1952 and the suspension of normal political life in Egypt, *al-Katib* was banned and the committee ceased its campaign for a time. Some members of the group, including its secretary, Yusuf Hilmi, were arrested and freed only after the July coup d'etat. Subsequent to the Free Officers taking power, Ansar al-Salam operated in a semilegal fashion, meeting quietly in people's houses. The group did not want to provoke Nasser in the early days of his rule by flaunting independent sources of political activity.[32]

Peace committees spread to towns and villages throughout Egypt, but the movement did not penetrate deeply into the society. Rather, its strength was concentrated mainly among intellectuals and only secondarily among the leaders of the trade union movement. Still, as a means of expressing anti-British sentiment among the more politicized Egyptian patriots, Ansar al-Salam served an important function.

The Clash of Personalities and Principles

If the communists were able to leave an imprint on Egyptian society in the nationalist, intellectual, and labor arenas, the process was not an easy one. They faced considerable difficulties, some generated from inside their own ranks, others with origins from outside. One of the most crippling problems for the communist movement was factionalism.

In 1946, the revolutionary left had experienced the euphoria of sharing in important and effective activity through the National Committee of Workers and Students. Once the intoxication generated by the nationalist militancy had worn off, the revolutionary left suffered a painful political hangover. Dissatisfaction with the pace and direction of the newly formed DMNL, personality clashes, unfulfilled political aspirations, ideological differences, and police strikes led to dissension within the group. In particular, the DMNL's leadership was charged with assenting to an "unprincipled" unity, which meant essentially that the issues of policy, organization, and leadership had not been rigorously or democratically worked out in advance and that explicit documents which could have averted damaging factionalism were absent.

The organization was condemned to months of impotence partly because it failed to tolerate any dialogue or democracy within it. Differences of opinion were simply not accepted and when disagreements arose the recourse was to expulsion or resignation rather than compromise or discussion. Sharif Hatata commented:

> I think essentially that people . . . did not have the experience and knowledge of . . . inner party struggle. Suppose a minority . . . didn't accept the decisions of the central committee or started a factionalist newspaper . . . you can let it go that way for some time. You accept the situation and move slowly toward clarification. Things take time and effort. . . . You can live with factions . . . in the hope that things will regularize themselves.[33]

In fact, in 1948 things were anything but regularized. The Palestine War had broken out and arrests of communists came fast on the heels of martial law, leaving only a few leaders outside the prison walls. Compounding the police problems were ideological differences between the incarcerated "old guard" and the still free rank and file. Moreover, Ahmad Husayn established the non-communist but possibly rival Socialist Party and the rule of the minority political parties signaled a defeat for constitutionalism and open political discourse in Egypt.

With the spirit of cooperation lacking, more than a dozen organizations—offshoots of the DMNL—appeared on the political scene between 1948 and 1950, most being of a very transient nature. Undisguised conflict within the movement centered on several key issues, among the most prominent were: the communist position on Palestine and the overall ethnic composition of the movement; the viability of a united front with noncommunist organizations, especially the Wafd; and the "line of the democratic forces" carried over from the EMNL.

The Palestine War

In February 1947 the British government referred the Palestine question to the United Nations which then appointed a special committee to visit Palestine, appraise the circumstances, and report on its findings. The plan for partitioning the country into two independent parts, one Arab and one Jewish, was promoted and received a necessary majority in the General Assembly on November 29, 1947, with the Soviet Union, the United States, and France in agreement. Great Britain abstained. The proposal, however, met with a wave of indignation in the Arab world; Arab governments refused to sanction the loss of any Arab territory.

The Soviet Union supported partition in 1947 when in the past it had condemned Zionism as an imperialist ideology. This reversal in position was due, at least in part, to the Russian hope that division in the region would weaken the British militarily and politically.[34] Also, the Soviet Union expected the new Jewish state to respond favorably to communist, anti-imperialist, and Marxist ideology, and to demonstrate support for Russia in appreciation for the latter's support for partition.[35]

The leadership of the Egyptian communists took note of the Russian action and followed its example by also endorsing the partition plan. This led to charges from both the Egyptian government and the Palace that Egypt's left was subservient to the Russian Communist Party and to the virtual equation of communism with Zionism.

Actually, consideration of the Palestine situation in Egypt predated the outbreak of war. Indeed, radical Egyptians had been thinking about Palestine for perhaps a decade, and Jewish communists were particularly attentive to the problem. In order to counter any trend toward Zionism, Marcel Israel founded the Jewish League to Combat Zionism (al-Rabita al-Israiliyya li Mukafahat al-Sahyuniyya) in the mid-1940s. The League, though quickly taken over by Iskra and headed by Ezra Harari, had a wider membership and included leftists and communists alike. In a statement which took the form of a pamphlet entitled "Against Zionism—In the Interest of Jews and In the Interest of Egypt," the League noted four objectives in its battle against Zionism. They included working against Zionism; strengthening ties between Egyptian Jews and the Egyptian people in the struggle for independence; lessening the gap between Jews and Arabs in Palestine; and solving the problem of the wandering Jew. The League was short-lived. Prime Minister Nuqrashi dissolved the group in 1947. Some conjectured that the closure resulted both from Nuqrashi's fear of the combined efforts of Arabs and Jews working against imperialism and from Nuqrashi's own links with very rich Jewish businessmen in Egypt who held Zionist sympathies.[36]

Most Egyptian leftists called for the acceptance of Israel within the limits of partition set down by the United Nations. Specifically, they called for the creation of an independent Arab state in Palestine, indemnification of the refugees, and the conclusion of a peace treaty with Israel.[37] Albert Arie commented on the communist position.

> From the beginning in Iskra and in the EMNL, then the DMNL, the members were absolutely against Zionism, against the further immigration of Jews to Palestine. They advocated a solution to the Palestine problem consisting of the common fight of Jews and Arabs against imperialism. They said to resolve the problem, first of all, the imperialists must leave Palestine—that meant the end of the Mandate. They advocated a democratic Palestine for all the inhabitants. Then a change occurred in 1947 . . . with Gromyko's speech in the General Assembly in which he approved the partition. . . . For the DMNL, the analysis was that there were now in Palestine two nations under formation and each had the right to self-determination. . . . Despite our radical opposition to

Zionism, we analyzed the fact that a Jewish nation was already in formation. Even if it was wrong in the beginning, it was a fact. We said that the best form would be a single state with two nationalities, but due to the historical situation, this single state option was difficult. As a result, there was no solution except partition. . . . Partition meant the end of the British Mandate and the evacuation of British troops. We thought that the formation of two states, one for each nation, could lead to the seeds of collaboration between these two states in the future. . . . What happened in 1948 was that the Israeli state was proclaimed but no Arab state was proclaimed.[38]

The DMNL's decision to support the partition plan was not, however, universally accepted by its membership. In consequence, there was an eruption of Egyptian-Jewish friction within the organization. In particular, Sid Sulayman Rifai, (an important member of the organization, once very close to Curiel, and later secretary-general of the group), pressed for the expulsion of Henri Curiel and Hillel Schwartz from the party because of their ethnic origins.[39] The leadership discussed the issue of the Jews in high-ranking positions; it disagreed with Rifai and gave both Curiel and Schwartz its vote of confidence. But the party was weakened internally as a result of the hostility which was generated.[40]

While the majority of the Egyptian population emotionally supported the Palestinian Arabs in the hope of keeping all of Palestine an integral part of the Arab Middle East, the revolutionaries of the DMNL who supported partition held a dissenting and unpopular view.[41] In an effort to defend and explain its position, *al-Jamahir*, the party newspaper, announced the following:

We do not want to take Palestine away from the Arabs and give it to the Jews, but we want to take it away from imperialism and give it to the Arabs and Jews. . . . Then will begin the long struggle for rapprochement between Arab and Jewish states.[42]

The revolutionary left also stated its opposition to the Palestine War because, in its analysis, it allowed repressive Arab regimes such as the one in Egypt to:

stop the trend of the rising nationalist movement and turn our holy war against the imperialist into a religious and racial war. . . .

The intent is to divert the attention of the toiling masses away
from the struggle for an improved standard of living to an outside
matter which neglects this battle.[43]

It has been asserted by the left that King Faruq used the war as
a means of restoring himself to the role of national leader. His intent,
according to the communists, was to direct popular feelings away from
local problems and toward the conflict abroad. By diverting the anti-
Zionist feelings of the Egyptians to his advantage, the left assumed
that the monarch could manage temporarily to erase his increasingly
negative image and boost the weakening regime. Monarchist rule, it
was argued, was given a temporary respite when the war engaged sections of the local nationalist movement in a racial war against Jews
and turned people's thoughts away from the antidemocratic government and imperialism.[44] It is unclear whether Faruq, in fact, calculated his actions in this way. Very likely, however, Faruq used the war
as a prop in order to appear as the leader of the Arab world and to
emerge as the stronger force in his battle for power with the Wafd and
other Arab forces.

In Egypt, the war also meant the imposition of martial law, the
resumption of antidemocratic measures, and the opening of concentration camps. It thereby provided the Palace with a choice opportunity to strike the leftists who were accused of national treason for
their stand on Palestine.

When martial law was proclaimed on May 15, 1948, a brutal
wave of internment of the revolutionary left began which seriously
immobilized communist activity. The widespread arrests struck at
the core of the movement, hitting first the leaders and then the members, and incalculably retarded its development. However, the campaign was not directed exclusively against the underground; it was
simultaneously intended to silence the growing dissatisfaction of the
working class which had been demonstrating its frustration through
strikes over the past year. A communist tract communicated the fury
of the left:

The tyrannical Nokrashy government has taken advantage of the
Palestine imbroglio to intern and disperse a number of workers
and their families and to cast many others in jail. The national
spirit is thus being domineered so as to satisfy the reactionary
imperialists. Martial law had been proclaimed simply to please
the British ally. . . . Truly the Nokrashy government has become

famous for its violation of the principles of justice, humanity and democracy.

Egyptians! Workers! The present regime does not represent you. You must, therefore, work to bring about its collapse![45]

Tensions ran high during the time of the Palestine conflict and violence erupted. The office of *al-Jamahir* was bombed as was the house of Henri Curiel. There were arrests, repeated house searches, and physical violence against some members of the DMNL.[46] Along with martial law came increased racial attacks against Egyptian Jews, committed principally by Muslim extremist groups. The resentment of the Muslim Brotherhood against Zionism was turned inward toward Egypt and partially fueled by intemperate monarchist declarations. The intolerable behavior of the Brotherhood led Nuqrashi to outlaw the group on December 8, 1948. On December 28, Nuqrashi was assassinated by a member of that society in retaliation; he was replaced by Ibrahim Abd al-Hadi who took over as head of the Saadist Party and prime minister in the government.

The most important effects of the Palestine War in Egypt were the internment of the left-wing opposition, widespread disappointment with the Arab failure, and the rupture of relations between army officers and the King. Egypt's humiliating performance in the war was due to military unpreparedness and domestic corruption. The country's defeat had a profound effect on public life as people learned about the inefficiency and corruption of the government, the scandals of the misappropriation of war funds, the stealing of military stores, and the neglect of the wounded. When the army realized that the King and his clique supplied imperfect and reduced price weapons and then took a cut of the profits, it felt betrayed by its own leaders.[47] Resentment against the government, in fact, roused some of the younger officers to form the Free Officers Movement.

An interesting note is that while the left vigorously protested the Palestine War, the conflict was not at that time seen as a focus for developing pan-Arab nationalism. The prevailing tendency inside the Egyptian communist movement was one of indigenous patriotism; the idea of placing Egyptian nationalism in a wider context of pan-Arabism was missing. In fact, it was highly unlikely that cosmopolitan Jewish communists or Egyptian communist intellectuals brought up in that tradition would have foreseen or espoused this trend. Since the communists were trying to establish for themselves a place in local Egyptian society, they rarely looked to the Arab population be-

yond the Egyptian borders. What was needed was a truly native in-
gredient, and one coming from outside the communist movement;
this developed with Gamal Abdul Nasser's far-reaching notion of nationalism.[48] Ismail Sabri Abd Allah, who played an important role
in the communist movement in the 1950s, confirmed this assessment
when he stated:

> We felt solidarity with the Arabs but this feeling was not care-
> fully analyzed nor taken into consideration in our strategy. After
> all, we were the sons of the Egyptian bourgeoisie which since the
> 1920s sided away from the Arab nation.[49]

The Policy of the Front

It was the DMNL's policy during the 1940s and 1950s to work toward
the establishment of a popular front when circumstances and events
permitted. This decision was taken despite disagreements among the
leadership—in this case most notably expressed by Sid Sulayman Rifai
and Sid Turk. The front was to take on the form of an alliance between groups of workers, peasants, the petty bourgeoisie, democratic
intellectuals, and the radical organizations and parties already in existence. The issues on which diverse individuals and groups could most
commonly agree were the support for democratic liberties, the improvement of the conditions of life for the masses, independence, and
world peace. Front activity developed in 1946 with the National Committee of Workers and Students, in 1951 with the guerrilla warfare
against the British in the Canal Zone, in the alliance of the Free
Officers, in the peace movement, and in the National Democratic
Front of 1954,[50] whose pressure may have contributed to the Revolutionary Command Council's decision to dissolve itself.[51]

The purpose of the front was to give underground political organizations, especially, the experience of legal and nationalist activity and to provide links between open and clandestine work.[52] However, it was also meant to demonstrate that the fusion of unrelated
groups into an alliance working collectively toward a common objective could make an impact on the affairs of the state.[53] The most
immediate struggle was against the British. *Al-Malayin* (The Millions),
an organ of the DMNL, stated in 1951 that "the only way to fight
imperialism is through armed struggle and armed struggle is only

possible through unifying all popular forces in a united front prepared for that struggle."[54] It called on the Muslim Brotherhood, the
Socialist Party, nationalists, Wafdists, workers, and students to join
together to fight Anglo-American imperialism and support democratic
freedoms.

For front activity to be successful, however, there had to be an
accepted leadership that forged ahead in political thinking and took
the other members and groups with it. According to Sharif Hatata,
the infrequency of cooperative work in Egypt was due to the fact that:

> None of these organizations could be the pioneer political leader-
> ship, none could crystalize political thinking in such a way as to
> draw with them the other movements. Political thinking is not
> something you can impose; it comes because you are more far-
> sighted, clearer.[55]

Shared activity occurred only infrequently, also, because the different groups were for the most part bitter opponents. Until 1949, both
Ahmad Husayn's Young Egypt and the Muslim Brotherhood were denounced by the DMNL as fascist. Ahmad Husayn was even accused
of being a British agent. The situation changed when the communists,
the Muslim Brothers, and the Young Egyptians were imprisoned together. They got to know and talk to one another—and a dialogue was
begun which continued even after their release. In 1950, Ahmad Husayn's party became the Socialist Party, and a wing of the Muslim
Brotherhood called for collaboration with communists against imperialism.[56]

The Line of the Democratic Forces

There was considerable internal criticism regarding Curiel's "line of
the democratic forces" by those who wanted to establish an orthodox
Egyptian communist party. The controversial idea on which Curiel
insisted was that radically-minded people living in an occupied and
developing country should first concentrate on establishing a democratic movement of national liberation with a Marxist center and a
Marxist awareness and only afterward form a communist party. Curiel's
opponents insisted that his position was flawed and, as a result, that

the DMNL concentrated too heavily on the nationalist cause almost to the exclusion of socialist goals.

This disagreement highlighted an important dilemma felt by many communists both inside and outside Egypt. Specifically, it focused on how internationalists, whose concerns theoretically touched the entire world population, reconcile both the nationalist movement and questions of a nationalist nature. Particularly in the case of Egypt, where the British presence was still felt, the communists debated whether socialism or national independence should take priority in the movement. This issue was never satisfactorily resolved by the Marxist left itself.

Factionalism within the Democratic Movement for National Liberation

As early as February 1948 there was an explosion in the DMNL detonated by one of its members, Shuhdi Atiya al-Shafii, who played an important part in breaking down the organizational unity of the group. Along with others, al-Shafii was troubled by the acceptance of the Palestine partition plan, the adoption of the "line of the democratic forces," the reluctance of the leadership to discuss strategy with the base, and the continued endorsement of a leadership which was disproportionately composed of cosmopolitan Jews.

Al-Shafii arranged meetings to discuss the situation and to try to win people over to his point of view. Students were receptive to his appeals and became the first to get involved. Al-Shafii wrote a report of about seventy pages identifying his objections to the DMNL. Entitled, "Here Is The Egyptian Communist Organization That We Wish To Create," the report criticized the communist movement for being bourgeois in composition and for being made up primarily of intellectuals, students, and the petty bourgeoisie. The DMNL, in particular, was faulted for being politically infantile and criticized for undertaking political activities of a Wafdist character. Identified as a movement of national democratic forces, it was charged with being "uniquely capable of weakening the class struggle by dispersing its militant forces over diversified fields of action."[57] The main activity, the report submitted, should be the organization of cells within the structure of a genuine Bolshevik party. According to the statement, the Bolshevik party should link socialist aspirations to the movement of the working class, primarily to the industrial proletariat in essential industries, who were expected to be the most politically advanced and the most open to socialist ideas. Students and revolutionary intellectuals, the report continued, should not be neglected for they constitute a revolutionary force in colonized countries having developed progressive traditions concurrently with the national struggle. The principal target of the national movement must be its fusion with the class struggle through agitation in the form of tracts, newspapers, trained agitators in strikes and demonstrations, and through nationalist propaganda tied to the daily economic aims of the masses. For this, the report stressed, a Bolshevik organization was essential.

Shuhdi Atiya al-Shafii's provocation led to the formation of the group, the Revolutionary Faction. From the perspective of al-Shafii, a former member of Iskra who was accustomed to a structured, almost conspiratorial organization, the DMNL had too flexible and open a structure. According to him, it lacked discipline, direction, goals; moreover, it would never rise above its limitations because of its Jewish leadership. Al-Shafii resented the cosmopolitan bias of the party at least partly because, although he was one of the first Egyptians promoted into the central committee of Iskra, he lost his position with the establishment of the DMNL.

Al-Shafii embraced Schwartz's theory of stages and witnessed the beginnings of change when Iskra had entered into its second phase of development during which Egyptian intellectuals were growing in number and position while the relative prominence of the cosmopolitan members was shrinking. People like al-Shafii had been on the rise in Iskra. That there were still Jews in the leadership of the DMNL in 1948 signaled, for them, a retreat to an earlier past.

Muhammad Sid Ahmad, himself active during this time, remembered the issues which produced this splinter group:

> What sticks in my mind is the point they [Shuhdi Atiya al-Shafii and Anwar Abd al-Malik] brought up that communism is being attacked as Zionism and that there is something wrong in that. The reason is that there has been a Jewish leadership which has been bookish, which is not linked with the tissue of the Egyptian realities. It was quite outspoken in its anti-Jewish stand to the extent that for a number of people . . . it might be anti-semitic a bit. It was a violent reaction against the feeling that the whole movement was held and perhaps manipulated by Jews and that

their commitment to Marxism was colored by things that might be alien to an authentic Egyptian Marxism. . . . The element of a Jewish leadership came out very prominently and the justification for breaking down the whole thing was centered around it. This was the Revolutionary Faction.[58]

Soon after the establishment of the Revolutionary Faction in February or March 1948, Shuhdi Atiya al-Shafii was arrested and imprisoned for several months. During the time he was incarcerated, the faction foundered and ultimately dissolved itself. One important point about the emergence of the Revolutionary Faction, however, is that it provoked new centers of opposition to surface which produced a split in the DMNL's leadership. Shuhdi Atiya al-Shafii's conflict with the leaders of the organization was the first trial in the DMNL's long history of factionalism.

After the formation of the Revolutionary Faction, other dissident groups emerged. (See Figure 4.) Some, like the DMNL-Revolutionary Workers, DMNL-Communist, Toward a Communist Party, the Vanguard of the Egyptian Communists, Toward a Bolshevik Organization, and Toward an Egyptian Communist Party were short-lived and relatively unimportant.[59] Yet another group, the Voice of the Opposition, did create serious cleavages in the Marxist movement and hence deserves special comment.

The Voice of the Opposition was a well organized and highly theoretical splinter group carved out of the DMNL by Odette and Sidney Solomon. Together, they formulated what became known as the ultraleftist line in communist circles. Their group was designed to be exclusively the party of the working class and not one of intellectuals. To that end, the organizers advanced the line that each member should go directly to the working class and recruit—even if this meant mass arrests. The leadership admitted to the perils of factionalism but insisted on forming a new organization which was based on democratic centralism. Ironically, in fact, the Voice of the Opposition was run in the most conspiratorial and dictatorial manner: the democratic objective never materialized.

Although its platform called for 100 percent workers in the organization, the Voice of the Opposition drew its membership mainly from the intellectual section of the DMNL and included students, minorities, and a significant number of women. When elections to the central committee were held in 1948, four leaders were chosen:

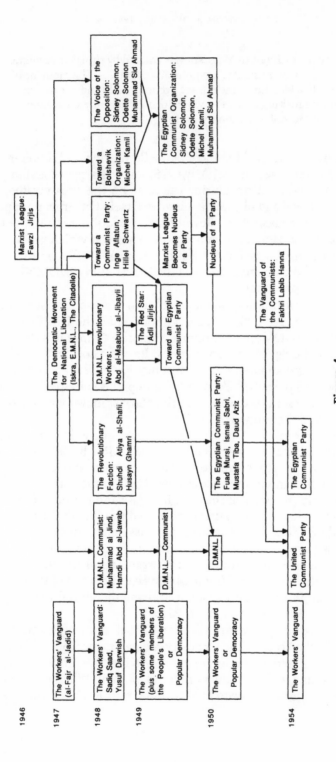

Figure 4

The Map of the Communist Movement

Sidney Solomon, Odette Solomon, Fatma Zaki, and Michel Kamil, (who was replaced by Muhammad Sid Ahmad when the former was arrested on January 14, 1949). None was from working class or even humble origins.

According to its strategic line, the group identified only one stage for the Egyptian revolution and that was the socialist revolution; unlike the theoretical assumptions of other groups, it ignored any need for a stage of bourgeois democracy. The organization published an analysis of Egyptian capitalism in which it stated:

> Nascent Egyptian capitalism has reached an agreement with colonialism. . . . This agreement allowed it to grow, tied together with colonialist monopoly. This interconnection took its final form in 1936 when Egyptian capitalism became linked to colonialism. Thus, Egyptian capitalism lost, once and for all, any claims to being a revolutionary force against colonialism. It betrayed the national cause and became a part of the camp of counter-revolution. Therefore, the national revolution must be directed against Egyptian capitalism. There is a direct contradiction between the interests of international colonialism and the interests of the Egyptian proletariat because the former blocks the working class from achieving its goal of socialism. . . . The working class is the only class that has the . . . capacity to lead the other national classes against colonialism . . . and for socialism.[60]

After the outbreak of the Palestine War, when disruption and chaos characterized the communist movement, Marxists in relatively large numbers joined the Voice of the Opposition, thereby strengthening its ranks in contrast to other communist groups. Not only did the "line" of the group appeal to many, but its leaders, Odette and Sidney Solomon, who were strong of character and theoretically oriented, were attractive role models. Muhammad Sid Ahmad, who knew the husband and wife team intimately, related:

> Sidney, he could generalize, theorize, become quite convincing in the presentation of things. But Odette was the real leader. . . . She was the one who got the glimpse of what should be done and she would move. Then Sidney would supply the theory. She was a young woman of very strong character. She used to say of herself, "I am a Stalinist 100 percent". . . . She would break everyone around her into pieces. . . . She smashed people of the greatest prominence.[61]

Muhammad Sid Ahmad was one of the young intellectuals who left the DMNL to work for the Voice of the Opposition. Coming from a distinguished and aristocratic family of pashas going back at least three generations, his communist activities were especially frowned upon. His father, who had substantial landholdings, was completely uninvolved in politics. Sid Ahmad remarked:

> He was of this category of people who looked down on politics. Even my uncle, Sidqi Pasha, who was a prominent and most conservative politician, a sort of Churchill figure—very clever and very reactionary, more royalist than the King, who defended the King's interests better than the King perceived them . . . was looked down upon as a minor branch of the family.[62]

In Cairo during World War II, Muhammad Sid Ahmad was enrolled in the *lycée français* along with other upper class Egyptian Muslims. Because of his facility for languages and his family's interest in his acquiring a thorough education, he pursued a combination French and Arabic baccalaureate. Muhammad was introduced to politics in the *lycée* through fellow students and radical instructors. He also attended lectures at the House of Scientific Research—but only for a short time. Anonymous letters were sent to his parents by the police, informing them of their son's activities. When confronted by his father, Sid Ahmad was forced to deny his involvement in radical politics because he was already organized in an underground cell and could not divulge his communist affiliation.

Through police contacts, the family's watchful chauffeur who shadowed him, and reports made by family friends, information about his political activity was passed to his father who tried various ways of separating his son from his radical interests. He even sent him abroad in the hope that distance and a hearty dose of amusement might cure Sid Ahmad of his youthful derelictions. His father failed, however, to alter his son's beliefs.

Muhammad Sid Ahmad remembered his experiences of the time:

> My parents decided to send me away—I was doing Engineering at the time—to finish my studies in Birmingham. So I went to Odette and said, "What should I do?" She and Sidney agreed, suggesting, "Accept the offer to travel and come back." I was sent to France first to become a spoiled boy with a lot of money. . . . I spent

two months in Paris . . . and then I took a plane back to Egypt but told nobody. My parents thought I had gone to the Soviet Union; and I disappeared for two years. I never went to England. Instead, I went underground and moved into an apartment with Odette and Sidney from which we never went out until we were arrested a year and a half later. The period when we lived in one room was a very hard one. . . . I was accused all the time of being opportunistic, of doing the one big courageous act and that was coming back, but I was not able to stand up to that level of sacrifice. . . . All our contact with the organization was through correspondence; we met nobody. . . . When we were arrested and I went to prison, it was as if I were liberated, psychologically speaking, to show you the atmosphere.[63]

The Solomons did, by the standards of the time, take extreme security measures, hiding themselves in an apartment from the announcement of martial law on May 15, 1948, until 1950 when, together with Muhammad Sid Ahmad, they were arrested. Accordingly, the center of power of the organization became a few people in a locked room who sent correspondence and directives out through messengers and carriers. Instructions covered those both inside and outside of prison. Careful attention was paid to party members and even after arrests were made and people were incarcerated, reports came in identifying how members behaved in jail, and whether they respected the discipline of the organization.

It did not take long before even the most committed and well intentioned members drifted away or were expelled from the organization. Gradually, the other groups were sustained by the people who left the Voice of the Opposition, (called, in 1949, the Egyptian Communist Organization): the DMNL, especially, grew in numbers while support for the Solomons waned considerably. The following example demonstrates conclusively the declining interest in the group. On January 1, 1949, some 500 members were organized. After three months, 250 of them had been arrested. One year later, only ten members were left.[64] Muhammad Sid Ahmad explained how this happened:

The party required people to try to recruit among workers. You can just imagine young Jewish girls from the center of Cairo going to Shubra al-Khayma under martial law and without any experience. People ended up being arrested. In practical terms it was a kind of suicidal line.[65]

In truncated form, the Egyptian Communist Organization hung on until the early 1950s when the leadership was arrested and imprisoned.[66]

The Resurgence of the Marxist and Nationalist Movements

Impotence and internal divisiveness characterized the communist movement at the end of the 1940s. But the factionalism which so deeply weakened Marxism in Egypt also proved to have positive consequences. In a productive way, division forced the broader movement to re-evaluate and even criticize itself. It demanded self-assessment at least in an effort to control its deviants. It pointed to the isolation of the communist movement from the core of society and highlighted the need for wider recruitment. Factionalism encouraged a greater degree of regimentation, tighter security, and a heightened sense of party discipline. But the negative effects were certainly damaging: the ultraradicalism and perpetual isolation and sectarianism present in the late 1940s contributed to police arrests, imprisonment, and ultimate powerlessness.

Although the latter 1940s constituted a dark period for Egyptian communism, the dawn of the 1950s marked a dramatic improvement in the spirits, expectations, and activities of the members of the communist underground. This was, to a large extent, occasioned by the return of the Wafd to power in January 1950 in the last truly free general election in Egypt's modern political history; by the release of numerous political prisoners from the camps and prisons; and by a more open political atmosphere. Once again, conditions became ripe for a renewal of aggressive political activity. The nationalist and anticolonialist movements were reactivated, the university campuses were alive with political militancy, workers' strikes multiplied throughout the country, the peace movement rallied, and the communist movement was again building up its forces in an effort to capture at least some of the vitality of the popular movements.

Anglo-Egyptian relations were not at this time at all amicable, and a speedy end to the occupation did not look promising. The British forces in Egypt numbered 30,000, three times the number allowed by the 1936 Treaty. The British, themselves, wanted an agreement but could not ignore the strategic importance of the Suez Canal area. It was Britain's contention that the zone was the most suitable place to locate a British base: in the event of war, it could be expanded to allow for a major British campaign in the Middle East.

Al-Nahhas rejected the English idea of continuing the presence of British troops in the Canal Zone and he opposed the suggestion that the base become an "allied" location housing both the British and the Americans. He wanted to win complete evacuation and would accept nothing less. When the hope of a settlement faded, al-Nahhas, in October 1951, declared the 1936 Treaty to be null and void. Al-Nahhas went on record in favor of total and immediate evacuation and the unification of the Nile Valley.[67] The opposition was unleashed and for the next three months it dominated the political scene. The mainstream of the Wafd lost control of the events as tension mounted in a population which called for the final removal of British troops from Egyptian soil.

The Suez Canal Zone—the last physical vestige of the occupation—was the focus of the nationalist movement. While the zone was located within Egyptian national boundaries, it had been all but relinquished to the British occupation forces after 1936 when British military installments on the site were built up. When the anti-British guerrilla movement emerged in 1951, it was determined to change the existing situation in favor of Egypt. The opposition took the form of something of an alliance between the communists, the Muslim Brothers, the Socialist Party, and the Wafdist Vanguard. Applying the tactic of the united front, anti-establishment left and right-wing political forces engaged in the Battle of the Canal Zone which was waged between October 1951 and January 1952. Cooperation between the various political groups was made possible through contacts which were first established when the opposition elements met inside the prison camps between 1948 and 1950.

The termination of the 1936 Treaty precipitated the concerted activity. Demonstrations raged in the larger cities. Guerrilla warfare broke out in the Suez Canal base and, in Ismailiyya for instance, militants acted in earnest: demonstrators struck the storehouses of the English post exchanges of the British army, navy, and air force, shots were exchanged, and armored vehicles dotted the city. In answer to an appeal from the Wafdist government, 80,000 Egyptian workers and office employees left their relatively high paying British affiliated jobs, thus paralyzing the workings of the Suez Canal base. Additionally, workers deserted British factories throughout the country. Railway workers, customs officials, airline employees, and longshoremen refused to handle British supplies. Tradesmen refused to honor their business contracts. Meanwhile, in Cairo and Alexandria, battalions of "freedom fighters" were organized. These included many students, workers, and intellectuals belonging to the Muslim Brotherhood, the left-wing of the Wafd, the communist movement, and the Socialist Party.

While most political groups were recruiting special forces from the larger urban areas to fight, the DMNL tried, through its limited contacts in the villages, to attract peasants to the national struggle. The result was that close to the Canal itself, a small number of peasants were recruited, given arms and ammunition from the army, and trained by some members of the Free Officers who were tied to the guerrilla movement.[68]

The freedom fighters, or *fidayun*, planned to strike the occupation forces from four directions in order to:

1—destroy the storehouses, depots, and supply pumps of the British
2—cut the lines of communications
3—disrupt supplies and prevent resupply
4—make the life of the occupation forces miserable[69]

On January 19, 1952, the battle came to its height when the Egyptian commandos struck at Tell al-Kabir. In response, the British commander-in-chief, General Erskine, ordered counter measures and attacked the Bulaq Nizam, the Egyptian auxiliary police force, largely composed of poor peasants. The commander of the Egyptian forces telephoned to Cairo, to the Minister of the Interior, Fuad Siraj al-Din, for instructions. Siraj al-Din ordered the Egyptian troops to engage the British and to resist at any cost. A twelve hour battle ensued during which the Bulaq Nizam were massacred.

When the news of the carnage reached Cairo, great crowds massed in front of the Cabinet offices in protest. Workers, students, intellectuals, and soldiers demonstrated in open challenge to the government and to the British. On Saturday, January 26, a general strike closed all factories in the country. Students from the universities and al-Azhar marched on the center of Cairo and joined forces with workers gathering from the suburbs. But before noon, violent and destructive street action took over. The business district of Cairo, with its foreign owned stores, restaurants, cafes, cinemas, hotels, and businesses, was set ablaze. Fuad Siraj al-Din announced the imposition of martial law, suspended the Constitution, censored the press, and ordered the arrest of about 250 people.

The guerrilla warfare in the Canal Zone and the subsequent street violence in Cairo momentarily unhinged the occupation. Moreover, it underscored once again Egyptian impatience with the British presence. For the members of the underground, the conflict was especially significant because it further destabilized an already shaky regime. Pointing to the King's declining popularity and the Wafd's lack of control, the fighting leveled a challenge at the entire structure of Egyptian hierarchies which had again proved incapable of effectively dealing with the British.[70]

Ultimately, however, the effect of the uprising against the British was limited. Hardly constituting a unified force, the various *fidayun* factions suffered from lack of preparation and experience. They were deficient in arms, ignorant of the local terrain, and for the most part strangers to the Canal Zone itself. There was no united leadership under which a truly popular front type movement might have organized. Rather, small bands of individuals, usually from the larger urban areas, made forays into British controlled territory with instructions from an immediate superior acting independently within a single political organization. In the main, local peasants were isolated from the battle which they, in fact, were better equipped to wage. As a result, the conflict was essentially limited to *fidayun* who, although they embraced the cause ideologically, could not devise the organizational, political, or strategic methods necessary to lead the potentially revolutionary situation.

While the guerrilla movement was small in numbers, it did generally reflect the widespread social and political discontent which crystallized after 1950. And yet, at this time, there was no organization in Egypt capable of coherently marshalling popular disaffection and directing it against the political hierarchy in a well conceived plan to oust the King, the British, and the ruling parties from power. A case in point is the revolutionary left, which had regrouped and had begun to engage in dissident activity, legally, through the peace movement, the press, and nationalist agitation. Its actions, however, were designed not to overthrow the government, but to highlight its vulnerability and its relative impotence. In consequence, it did no more than momentarily vex the government, for its strength was limited and its self-confidence shaky.

The leftists, who in 1946 had experienced both triumph and defeat from the National Committee of Workers and Students, did not learn from this experience. There was no serious analysis of why and how the 1946 events happened, how they could have been exploited more effectively, who was responsible for the defeat, and how future mistakes could be overcome. An optimal time to study the lessons of the past and to determine what should be done in the future to avoid past errors presented itself from 1948 to 1950 when numbers of militants were incarcerated in prisons and concentration camps. However, this situation was not utilized. As a result, when the revolutionary left engaged in the Canal warfare in 1951, it repeated the same mistakes it made in 1946.[71]

The Establishment of a New Group—
The Egyptian Communist Party

In 1945, a number of Egyptian students who were to be active in left-wing politics in the 1950s and beyond, traveled to Paris to continue their advanced education. Many were Jewish Egyptians, but a few were of native Egyptian origin. Fuad Mursi, Ismail Sabri Abd Allah, and Mustafa Safwan, (the son of one of the founders of the first Egyptian Communist Party in 1922), were among the latter group. While in Paris, all followed the developments of the Egyptian communist movement with avid interest. Most had contacts with the French Communist Party through Raymond Aghion, an expatriate Egyptian living permanently in Paris. Raymond Aghion was a relative of Henri Curiel and was involved with him in the Egyptian antifascist movement in the mid-1930s. After World War II, Aghion emigrated to France, became a member of the French Communist Party, and was responsible for recruiting Egyptian students in Paris. He also worked in the Party's Colonial Bureau which was led by Eli Mignot from 1946 to 1978. Fiercely anti-Curiel, Mignot tried to influence the direction of the Egyptian communist movement through the Egyptians living in France.[72] Mignot was especially close to Sabri Abd Allah, who was a key figure in the group and was working toward a doctorate in economics in Paris at the time.

Ismail Sabri Abd Allah was born in 1924 in a small village in Middle Egypt into a family of landowners. His father was *umda* of the village, an inherited position in the family.[73] Although not educated beyond the village school, his father inspired his son's intellectual interests and cultural development which culminated in his winning a scholarship to study in Paris. His was a politically minded family; his father was a Wafdist, two of his brothers were dismissed from the university in the 1920s and 1930s for their militantly nationalist behavior, and Ismail Sabri himself participated in Wafdist demonstrations from the age of fourteen. While a secondary school student in Cairo during the war when diplomatic relations were established with the Soviet Union, he began to learn about socialism. Through left-wing books which were available in downtown Cairo and primarily aimed at the Allied forces stationed there, Ismail Sabri familiarized himself with the Marxist tradition. He noted:

> I remember that my first contact with Marxism was through a popular series called the Little Lenin Library published by the British Communist Party. Also, I started reading the Allied press which included many things about communism, socialism and Marxism. This was a new discovery which coincided with the time I started to ask myself about the political line of the Wafd Party and its efficiency as a promoter of national independence. This helped transform my impressions or feelings about social phenomena into political consciousness. At fifteen or so I was very shocked when I learned that in my village we used to pay a higher price to hire an ass than a laborer for the fields. I even remember the figures—a man would get eight piasters a day while an ass cost ten. This was terribly shocking for me.[74]

At the university, Ismail Sabri began to clarify his political ideas and when he discovered the social dimensions of the national movement his interest in political questions intensified. With his peers he talked about the Allied victory and the end of the British occupation; and together they participated in the nationalist demonstrations which were commonplace in the university. In 1946, he left Egypt to study in France, only intermittently returning until he completed his doctorate in 1951.

About the Egyptian students abroad with him, Ismail Sabri commented:

> The Egyptians who went to Paris . . . fell broadly into two categories: those who had the firm intention to return back to our country and those who planned to remain in Paris and this was the larger group. Of course the interests were not always the same. Those who intended to remain in Paris had a sentimental attach-

ment to Egypt but were more attentive to what was going on in Paris. And when you are detached from reality you tend to freeze this reality as you left it. You become a bit insensitive to change. The reality becomes remote, rigid, fixed. This is especially true in a country like ours where political changes happen fast, where political personnel change fast. . . . Our French Communist Party comrades even advised that those people who had no intention of returning to Egypt should drop any specific Egyptian activity and become involved in French life and the Party and help Egypt through international solidarity.[75]

It was not at all unusual that the Egyptian students had contacts with the local French Communist Party in the immediate postwar period. The democratic traditions they found abroad stood in marked contrast to their own political experiences in Egypt. Not surprisingly, the provocative and exciting intellectual currents which they encountered aroused them, pointed to the fact that Egypt was democratic in form only, and caused them to reflect and even become skeptical. Referring to the relations between the Egyptian students and the French Communist Party, Ismail Sabri continued:

In the post-war period, and before the Cold War, there was a spirit of internationalism. It was quite natural that foreigners would belong to a local communist party. I was fascinated by the liberal, democratic game. In my country, communism was anathema and here in France the first party [to top the list] by electoral vote was the Communist Party. This was a joy for me. The period was very active intellectually with stories and poetry about the resistance and struggles against imperialism. This was a glorious time. At this time, the Communist Party was a major party; it was by no means in the ghetto. Most of the greatest intellectuals in France were communists or friends of the Communist Party.[76]

The French Communist Party's Colonial Bureau grouped the Egyptian radicals in Paris into a general association without regard to a member's prior organizational affiliation or particular ideological predisposition. Called Le Groupe des Égyptiens, and led by Ismail Sabri Abd Allah, the group could never function as an homogeneous and unified body. Instead, from the beginning, there were political divisions which reflected and were reinforced by the factionalism present in the Egyptian communist movement itself.[77]

Well established by May 1948, the group began focusing on two issues of emotional and practical importance: the divisions in the communist movement reinforced by the Palestine War, and the heightened campaign of arrests simultaneously directed against the communists by the government. With its veteran leadership interned, and an inexperienced, highly fragmented younger guard in control, the movement was, at least temporarily, eviscerated. Fuad Mursi was keenly aware of the situation. He stated:

> When in France we discussed the state of things [in Egypt], we reached the conclusion that it was high time we had a communist party in Egypt. This discussion took place with the French Communist Party . . . and with Mustafa Safwan . . . and Ismail Sabri Abd Allah. . . . We wrote to our friends in Egypt . . . to do their best to form a communist party in Egypt.[78]

Meanwhile, concrete steps were being taken to achieve that goal. In July 1948, Ismail Sabri returned to Egypt for the summer holidays. While in the country he contacted various communist organizations, presenting himself as a delegate mandated by the French Communist Party to try to unify the different groups. Although not successful in actually setting up a unified group, he did manage to circulate the idea of unification. In January 1949, Fuad Mursi finished his doctoral studies and returned to Egypt. It proved to be his task to stir up the Egyptian communist movement and inject new life into it. According to his own testimony, he was:

> more or less authorized by our French comrades to begin discussions on the spot in Egypt with those of the DMNL not in prison or in concentration camps. I tried to contact every kind of communist organization . . . to advise them to unite to form a single party.[79]

Mursi's intention was not only to unify the left but to create a new organization, unscarred by the antagonisms and misunderstandings of the past, untainted by past factionalism, unburdened by past leadership.

Fuad Mursi had something of an unusual background for an Egyptian communist. Born in Alexandria in 1925, he came from a humble family. His father was a worker in the railways who had achieved some standing in the industry so that his family home was not a poor one. At a young age, Fuad Mursi admired the Wafd Party and was also interested in the anti-British political writings of the Misr al-Fatat group. While a student in the Law Faculty at Alexandria University, he began studying Egyptian history, the Quran, Islamic Law, Arabic literature, and general political science. During the war years he also became acquainted with Marxist works through books brought to Egypt by British soldiers. Of his own political development Mursi said:

> I began adhering to Marxism because I found in it the answers to both questions which were raised by our national movement in Egypt: the British occupation and the treason of the upper classes including the disparity of income distribution. Everything that was raised about Egyptian society at that time I found answers in Marxism.[80]

Roughly simultaneous with Mursi's return to Egypt, a group of dissatisfied members of the DMNL or its splintered branches was meeting apart from the parent organization. Early in 1949, the members contacted Mursi and were receptive to his idea of establishing a party independent of the existing organizations. After months of meetings and preparatory work, a new group, the Egyptian Communist Party (ECP), was declared by Mursi in early 1950.[81]

Because Mursi and Sabri Abd Allah were absent from Egypt during the later 1940s when the nationalist movement was vibrant and nationalist ferment led to the partial unity of the communist movement, their efforts to found a new organization were criticized in some circles. The argument, made essentially by those attached to the DMNL, was that it was from a distance—from Paris—that they were viewing Egyptian communism, its flaws, and its strong points. Their detractors believed that they had no intention of unifying the movement, but instead had always meant to start afresh and to form a group with no history or positive attachment to the past. When the "Paris" students returned home, their efforts seemed to impugn communists already working in Egypt, and to suggest that they were beginning to create the communist movement in Egypt—that nothing had, in fact, existed previously. This, of course, alienated and angered a significant portion of the movement and led to the charge of "spoiler" leveled against Mursi and Sabri for not even attempting to work within the existing structure of clandestine politics.

With the establishment of the ECP in 1950, Fuad Mursi attempted a thorough, materialist analysis of the structure of Egyptian society and how to bring about change in a study entitled *The Development of Capitalism and Class Struggle in Egypt*. The report was divided into two parts, the first dealing with the development of the revolutionary movement in Egypt from the French campaign until 1948; the second setting out the immediate tasks before the communist movement.[82] According to the author, Egypt was categorized as a semifeudal, semicolonized country. The immediate battle to be waged was the national democratic revolution whose object was the removal of imperialist domination from the country. The working class, petty bourgeoisie, peasants, and progressive intellectuals were targeted as the forces of the revolution. The large landowners, capitalists of foreign origin who took refuge in imperialism, and the national bourgeoisie were considered traitorous to national liberation.

Mursi's economic study focused, among other things, on class differentiation, the emergence of the Egyptian bourgeoisie, and the embourgeoisement of some landowners. He noted that there was a growing capitalist class in Egypt which stemmed from mixed origins: from the bureaucracy, with lawyers and engineers particularly active, and from the rural rich, either from the educated sons of the middle landowners or the educated sons of the landowning peasants. Since foreigners basically controlled much of the local Egyptian commercial and financial activity, very few indigenous capitalists emerged from this field. According to Mursi, democratic ideas were not very deeply rooted among the Egyptian bourgeoisie. Their landowning or bureaucratic backgrounds thwarted the practice of freedom and encouraged, on the contrary, domination from above. This pattern differed from the European experience where political freedom was linked to freedom of trade and it was the industrialists and traders who defended both.[83]

The Egyptian working class, Mursi argued, was strong enough to justify the establishment of a communist party. He reached this conclusion by identifying the various levels of working class consciousness. He considered the "professional" unity of the working class, which expressed itself in the trade unionist movement, the first layer of radical awareness. Above this, he identified the stage of political consciousness whereby the working class defended not only its own interests but those of other classes as well; the National Committee of Workers and Students in 1946 was an example of this. Both stages, he asserted, could unfold spontaneously and were, indeed, present in the Egyptian working class. But the highest stage of development, that of socialist consciousness, needed a sophisticated vanguard which could lead the workers and teach them about socialism. This was the role of the political party and specifically the communist party. Hence, his strong support for the establishment of the Egyptian Communist Party.

As secretary-general of the ECP, Fuad Mursi's theories carried considerable weight and the ideas he expressed were embraced by those surrounding him. According to his studies of landownership patterns, there were remnants of feudalism in Egypt. A few landowners owned great estates, some peasants held small plots of land, and the vast majority of the rural population were landless peasants. This led him and the party to support extensive peasant reform; this demand was radically more transformative than an agrarian revolution which brought technical and not social change. His conception of change in Egypt required the confiscation and subsequent distribution of large estates to poor peasants. But like the whole of the communist movement, the weakest point of the ECP was activity in the countryside.

Although, practically, the party recruited members of bourgeois and petty-bourgeois origin, and primarily students and intellectuals, theoretically, it counted on the working class to lead and guide the socialist revolution as part of an alliance with other classes. Specifically, working class fusion with the radical petty bourgeoisie of rural background was intended. Mursi categorized as petty-bourgeois a peasant who owned a plot of land which he could cultivate together with his family or in some cases with the assistance of hired labor. The ECP believed it essential to gain the support of this middle peasant because of his prominence and influence in the countryside. There was an impression that the middle-level peasant was the natural leader of the landless. It was through the offer of land and liberty that the party hoped to attract middle peasants to the organization.[84]

The party's theoretical framework borrowed from Lenin and Stalin where appropriate. In connection with the theories dealing with the national bourgeoisie, the ECP posited that the Wafd would participate in the nationalist movement against imperialism because it wanted unencumbered control over the economy and the independence from foreign control that went along with it. Once the nationalist revolution was won, however, the bourgeoisie would pass over to the reactionary camp and work against progressive forces. Accordingly, the decision was taken to isolate and oppose this class and the Wafd Party which represented it.

Saad Zahran, an early member of the ECP, commented:

We accepted the Stalinist point that the grand bourgeoisie was
not nationalist and therefore could not be allies. Instead, we said
that our allies must be the poor and middle-level peasants and
workers. We saw the Wafd as the client of imperialism and we
opposed the other communist groups that wanted to make an alliance with it. Our interest was to lessen the Wafd's effect especially on the peasants.[85]

A book which also had a profound effect on the members of the
ECP and which corroborated the Stalinist view was Mao Tse Tung's
New Democracy. Mao stated that the bourgeoisie in China was involved in the nationalist cause when the Japanese invaded the country, but could not be relied upon to support the socialist revolution;
in fact, the class ultimately became adversarial and joined the anti-
revolutionary camp. The Egyptian communists reflected on the experience of their Chinese counterparts when they rejected alliance with
the national bourgeoisie.

Organizationally, the party was made up of local cells in one's
neighborhood or place of work; unlike the DMNL, organization was
not based on gender, ethnic background, or professional status. The
area committee formed the next layer of the organization. At this level,
party members with responsibility for a number of neighborhood cells
carried out policy, maintained organizational discipline, controlled
education, and administered finances. The regional committee, which
stood above the area units, was followed by the "conference," which
consisted of representatives from the regional levels. From this group,
the central committee of three people was elected. The central committee, the highest body of the party, decided on strategies and tactics.

In contrast to other sections of the communist movement, the
ECP did not try to recruit the leadership of the labor movement, nor
penetrate into trade unions per se. Rather, it attempted to build secret workers' associations whose leaders were encouraged to work on
behalf of legal labor causes.[86] To its working class supporters, the ECP
emphasized social rights and the rights of the proletariat.

In the very early days of the party, a decision was taken to ex-
clude women and Jews from membership. The prohibition against
Jews—though short-lived—was initially based on a fear of internal contradiction over the establishment of the state of Israel, and on a desire

to ensure an indigenous leadership in the organization. Daud Aziz was prompted to comment:

> It is natural that in a backward country, the Marxist movement begins with foreign and intellectual elements. But it is not natural for foreigners to guide the political movement even if the movement is illegal and not known to the police. The Arab countries have their special traditions. The Arabic language, for example, is very difficult for foreigners to learn. Even if they learn it here [in an Arabic speaking country], the pronunciation is wrong. The ECP had no foreigners in the leadership positions and very few in the rank and file.[87]

Additionally, the ECP wanted to invalidate the government's characterization of the communist movement as morally shameful. In response, it instituted a ban against women joining the party in an apparent attempt to cleanse its reputation. The prohibition was lifted when the group recognized the utility of organizing women and the absurdity of both the government's charge and its own response. Thus, while the restrictions against women and Jews were once deemed appropriate to the situation by the policy makers, they were ultimately rescinded since they admittedly conflicted with the principles of Marxism and Leninism and could not be justified.

Soon after the establishment of the Egyptian Communist Party, 20,000 copies of its program were published and distributed to Egyptians active in political, intellectual, and journalistic affairs. The program was also published in the newspaper *Roz al-Yusuf* on April 17, 1951 and in the party's own organ, *Rayat al-Shaab* (The People's Banner), which was circulated both inside and outside the party. In addition, the party published a secret internal bulletin exclusively directed to its members called *al-Haqiqa* (Truth). About the group's journalistic activity, Ismail Sabri Abd Allah said:

> We had an underground paper and some of our comrades had infiltrated into legal newspapers. . . . Given the limited number of our membership we considered it adventurism to try to launch a weekly or monthly [open] paper. It would have made the identity of those working in it known to the police; the government would have closed it down after a time and the members would be listed as communists. We drew a very clear distinction between

underground activity and legal activity. . . . We published our own
organ, Rayat al-Shaab, and we managed against all odds to publish about 300 issues of it. It was done secretly with primitive
technology and hidden in small provincial towns. Authors submitted material and we sent it along to be printed and distributed. There was strict police control and so this was a very tough
thing to accomplish.[88]

The newspaper was distributed hand to hand, stuffed into the mail-
boxes of those sympathetic to the group's ideas, or sent by mail.

The ECP was set up essentially in opposition to the DMNL. In
contrast with the loose structure of the DMNL, the ECP insisted on
tight security and an "iron" organization. Although both groups called
for armed struggle against the British occupation, the ECP did not
send its members to the Canal Zone after abrogation of the 1936 Treaty
in 1951. While it did not prevent its cadres from participating as individuals in the Canal fighting, it saw the struggle in terms of a popular movement and not a party movement. The party tried to concentrate its resources on the existing regime and its allies in Cairo since
the capital was the center of things political. According to Fuad Mursi,
the enemy was not the British alone, but the whole regime which
included the King, his supporters, and the feudalists. Mursi asserted
that the left's exclusive concentration on the foreign occupation gave
native forces of reaction a free hand for repression.[89]

In an effort to reach outside the party, the ECP did establish ties
in 1951 with some members of Misr al-Fatat which by this time was
called the Socialist Party. Through Ahmad Husayn, (until he was arrested on January 26, 1952, accused of setting the fire that devastated
Cairo), and Sid Qutb, some joint public meetings were held and the
idea of a united front between the organizations was bandied about.
The ECP was supportive of establishing relations with the Nationalist Party of Fathi Radwan and with intellectuals like Ihsan Abd al-
Qadus who was then editor-in-chief of the newspaper Roz al-Yusuf.
United activity never materialized because of the ultimately disparate views of the various groups.

5

Communism and the Military Regime

The Military Comes to Power

In 1952 British soldiers were still in occupation of part of Egypt. Corruption abounded, and rising prices were accompanied by increased unemployment in urban areas. Conditions in the countryside were also deteriorating as a result of higher rents exacted from peasant farmers. The Wafdist leadership, once the barometer of the national movement, had by this time lost its vanguard role despite the fact that Ahmad Husayn as minister of social affairs, and Taha Husayn as minister of education, were inclined toward social reform in this period. A crisis of governing existed: no stable government could preside from above, and at the same time the society was in movement from below. The fabric of the regime was weak, and from January to July 1952 four Cabinets succeeded one another.

At this time, the revolutionary left or the Muslim Brothers could have become the heirs of political power in Egypt. Each was organized, politically conscious, and gaining in popularity.[1] Yet, both groups were unable to capture the moment. The revolutionary left, especially, was not set up to assume political power. It had not organized a mass movement, was still internally divided, tentative, and insecure. On its own, it was incapable of moving against the state. An alliance with other forces in the social and political arena was needed before any effective action could be contemplated. Crucially, the communists had yet to devise a concrete strategy for seizing power. Their mere advocacy of a national front, of strikes, demonstrations, and nationalist agitation was hardly sufficient. Unlike members of the military, when the communists spoke of force, they meant the force of numbers, the force

115

of the masses, and never the force of arms. In contrast to disaffected military officers, leftist dissidents did not encourage a military take-over.[2] That type of activity was left to the Free Officers, a small, secretive, politically diverse military group whose detailed strategy for toppling the monarchy was realized on July 23, 1952. Psychologically, the soldiers had few qualms about using force. In fact, their military training predisposed them favorably to the use of arms to resolve otherwise intractable political problems. The soldiers were, generally speaking, disciplined and conspiratorial, and seized an auspicious moment to overthrow the established regime.

The Free Officers who actually carried the day were not the military, nor the army as such, but a political movement within the military. This is a very important distinction. The Free Officer Movement was a kind of national front within the military in which all the opposition trends were represented—communists, Muslim Brothers, and Wafdists. The genius of Gamal Abdul Nasser was that he was able to gather around himself a group of officers who agreed on a limited number of points. The famous "Six Principles" expressed their views and was designed so that nothing in the manifesto conflicted with the direction of any of the organizations involved. They included:

- the elimination of imperialism and its collaborators
- the ending of feudalism
- the ending of the monopoly system
- the establishment of social justice
- the building of a powerful national army
- the establishment of a sound democratic system

Through this representative military opposition, Nasser ultimately took control of Egypt. Nasser required all those who worked with him to discipline their relations with their own political organizations to avoid security leakages. He did not ask his collaborators to give up their ideology, only to veil organizational ties behind allegiance to the Free Officers Movement. Khalid Muhyi al-Din, who was a founding member of the Free Officers, made this comment:

[When] we were underground, we wanted people to come to us. If we had said, "Cut your political relations" people would not have joined us. . . . There were those who were so committed to their political parties that they were unable to go on in the Free Officers. . . . We were not against ties at that time, but if those ties

were such that people took orders and this directed their activity
inside the Free Officers, then this was something else. . . . Nasser
wanted people to have contacts . . . in order to open the door to
more contacts. . . . Many kept their ties but had their loyalty to
the Free Officers.[3]

The structure of the Egyptian army itself, or more specifically
its class structure, also contributed to the officers' ability to seize
power. In particular, one of the results of the Anglo-Egyptian Treaty
of 1936 was that the Military College was opened to the nonaristo-
cratic, non-Turkish, Egyptian petty bourgeoisie and specifically to
those within this group who could afford to pay the £E60 tuition per
year, not an inconsiderable amount of money at the time.[4] Many of
the founding members of the Free Officers came from this social background and all of them entered the academy in the three years after
1936. New blood was injected into the army and with it came new
ideas. Khalid Muhyi al-Din recalled the period:

We began to study economics, world politics, subjects which had
never been taught at the Military College. Education and culture
started. The political climate in the country enriched the political consciousness of the officers. We became part of the national
movement.[5]

The Second World War brought a broader world view to Egyptians in
the military. Muhyi al-Din continued:

Anti-British feelings dominated the ideas of the officers especially
since there was a British mission in the army for training . . .
which issued secret reports about every corps. At that time there
was a pro-German sentiment in existence, not because of the
Nazis. . . . Germany was against England, we were against England,
so some believed that the defeat of England would help Egypt.
. . . When the defeat of Germany was clear and the brave fight of
the Soviets was known, the people began to realize what fascism
was. . . . From 1943, the officers tried to understand both world
and internal politics.[6]

Some of the political groups active in Egyptian society—the Muslim Brotherhood, Young Egypt, and the National Party which was
founded by Mustafa Kamil in the early 1900s and maintained a pres-

ence throughout Egypt's liberal era—were also operating within the military during the early 1940s. The EMNL began to recruit among non-commissioned officers during the war, but it was not until the formation of the DMNL that military membership in the communist movement became significant. The Wafd had less influence in the army at that time. This was the result of a number of factors. The military academy's admissions committee, which examined candidates before their matriculation, was under the direct control of the Palace and the minority parties. Consequently, most of those young soldiers chosen to enter the college were by design not adherents to the Wafd Party. To be sure, the Palace had always tried to control the military and keep it within its own sphere of interest—but the monarchy even went further, discrediting the Wafd whenever possible—with the result that few Wafdists were admitted into the Military College.[7]

The period 1944 to 1947 was one of reading and studying for those officers interested in national problems. Cells within the military were formed by the Muslim Brotherhood, the communists, and independent nationalists. Nasser himself tried to have contacts with and an understanding of the different trends on the scene, but he did not want to be a prisoner of one ideology. This was to serve his cause well when he organized in preparation for the coup d'etat.

The army had cause for dissatisfaction on both a national and military level. But the immediate detonator of the officers' anger was the Palestine War in which the Egyptian military fought without any preparation and with poor and sometimes even faulty equipment. That the King and his entourage made money on arms and ammunition contracts to the detriment of Egyptian soldiers was tantamount to national treason in the officers' eyes. The defective arms scandal coupled with the humiliating defeat in the war led directly to the formation of the Free Officers Movement in 1949.

Between 1950 and 1952, the group built strength and radicalized its members' national and social consciousness. Simultaneously, the press faulted the King and criticized the government, and the popular movement was showing renewed vitality. All of this contributed to the political understanding of the officers who became intimately involved in the national cause.

The cohesiveness of the Free Officers was the combined result of a shared past, school ties, combat experience, and their common hatred of the status quo. Having their social roots in the petty bourgeoisie, for the most part, meant that there was a certain cohesion to their group and an aversion to the traditional political parties from which they felt excluded and by which they felt betrayed. Organized and united, they could move decisively and preempt other political groups. In 1952 there was a power vacuum in the country and only a national liberation front, it seems, could take advantage of the situation. Nasser, through his military group, which was representative of the competing opposition trends in the country, succeeded in overthrowing the King and ushering in a new political era in Egypt.

The Relationship of the Democratic Movement for National Liberation with the Free Officers Movement

Perhaps because Nasser did not want to alienate the communists, or as a way of possibly neutralizing them, the DMNL was given advance knowledge of the coup d'etat through Ahmad Hamrush, leader of the DMNL's military branch, who was summoned to Cairo from Alexandria by Nasser on July 22. Nasser, according to Hamrush, briefed him on the events to take place and gave him an account of what needed to be done. Hamrush then passed the information on to Ahmad Fuad, Khalid Muhyi al-Din, and Sid Sulayman Rifai, secretary-general of the DMNL.[8]

The DMNL initially supported the Free Officers' coup because it was in favor of any action in the army which would first destabilize the old regime and then radically change it. Immediately after the officers' seizure of power, the communists considered it important to work with the new rulers in their effort to alter Egyptian society. Additionally, Ahmad Fuad of the DMNL was at that time considered to be one of the best advisors of Gamal Abdul Nasser, and the communists inside the army were thought to play an important role inside the Free Officers' group. Two prominent Free Officers, Abd al-Halim Amr and Yusuf Siddiq, were sympathetic to the ideas of the left, and both Ahmad Fuad and Khalid Muhyi al-Din regularly met with Nasser and discussed the policies of the Wafd, the struggles in the Middle East, the role of the United States, the King, the British, land reform, nationalization, and Palestine. In this way, Nasser was exposed to a leftist analysis of Egypt and the world. In short, the DMNL decided it would move with the revolution, all the while trying to inject Marxist attitudes into it.[9]

Because of its links with the Free Officers, the DMNL endorsed the coup and the initially progressive aims of its architects: the end of autocracy, liberation from imperialism, and the termination of feudalism. It defended what it saw as the democratic character of the army's actions, specifically, its relationship with the national democratic movement. Likewise, it supported the democratic ideals the officers promised to fulfill: the defense of the Constitution, the return to parliamentary life, the eradication of tyranny and corruption.

The DMNL considered the Free Officers a part of the national movement with its members sharing a communality of aims and aspirations. The communists established a relationship with the dissident Free Officers in 1950 through Khalid Muhyi al-Din, who fit neatly into both categories as a founding member of the Free Officers and a sympathetic Marxist. Khalid Muhyi al-Din's first organized ties to the communist movement began in 1947 when he joined Iskra. He was closely associated with Ali al-Shalaqani, (then a student activist), and Ahmad Fuad, (later, an important member of the Free Officers and a confidant of Nasser), but he remained involved in underground politics only until the outbreak of the Palestine War at which time he severed his ties to the organization. Simultaneously, his relationship with the people involved in communist activity lapsed. Between 1948 and 1950 he was taken up with military affairs and especially after 1949 with the Free Officers Movement.

In 1950 the relationship between Khalid Muhyi al-Din and Ahmad Fuad was reactivated when the DMNL decided to deepen the party's association with the military. By that time, there was already an established communist organization inside the army, created by the DMNL and headed by Ahmad Fuad and Ahmad Hamrush. It was the leadership's intention to set up a working alliance between the communist officers in the DMNL and the nationalist members of the Free Officers. Khalid Muhyi al-Din was considered the ideal conduit between the two groups. Muhyi al-Din stated:

> Ahmad Fuad asked me to come talk with him and make contact with him and some of the Free Officers. I prepared a meeting between him and Gamal Abdul Nasser and from that day started the link between the two groups. This was 1950. Ahmad Fuad was a member of the central committee of the DMNL. Through him came Ahmad Hamrush and others.[10]

The army organization inside the DMNL, which was called qism al-ahdhiya, (the shoe group), included members who joined the Free

Officers outright and others who worked with Nasser's circle but kept their political affiliation secret from the group. Muhyi al-Din explained:

> Some members of the DMNL group joined the Free Officers. We considered them members but their names were not known to Gamal Abdul Nasser. I told him there were some officers with relations to the communists. He said, "I don't accept communists, I accept officers. If they want to join . . . as officers, all right." Abdul Nasser was not ready to accept anyone as a communist; loyalty was first and foremost to be directed to the Free Officers. The cell remained in the DMNL but the men joined the Free Officers.[11]

Khalid Muhyi al-Din, himself, was never a member of the DMNL. He was an unaffiliated Free Officer who held independent leftist political ideas. Although he met regularly with Ahmad Fuad and had good relations with the organization, he prized his independence. As a Free Officer he did not pepper his discourse with communist slogans or dispense party propaganda. Instead, he said:

> I talked about democracy, land reform, economic reform, national and economic independence. I put forward aims which no one could refuse. I tried to preach my own ideas and the ground was fertile. . . . I did not represent the DMNL because I felt that this would weaken me. Although I was not part of the DMNL's political organization, our aims came together and this gave me more strength.[12]

For the DMNL, the affiliation with the Free Officers Movement was at the very least a means through which military information could be channeled to the communist group. Ahmad Hamrush confirmed this when he added:

> The decision was made to have . . . Khalid . . . supervised by Ahmad Fuad . . . have a connection with Gamal Abdul Nasser. We wanted to have special relations with him to know everything about the Free Officers.[13]

Because Hamrush was in charge of the military section of the DMNL, for security reasons he abstained from joining the Free Officers outright. But when he was trying to recruit officers into his secret movement, after being transferred to Alexandria from Cairo in 1951, he first introduced prospective candidates to the Free Officers Movement and then recruited them into the army section of the DMNL. Thus, Hamrush played the role of the Free Officer in order to attract new members into the DMNL.[14]

There was, in fact, a reciprocal relationship between the Free Officers and the DMNL's military organization. Those communist officers from the DMNL who were organized simultaneously as Free Officers reported military matters back to the organization and thereby kept the central committee apprised of pertinent information. The Free Officers, on the other hand, from 1950, depended on the DMNL to print their leaflets and address their envelopes, which contained Free Officer enclosures directed to military men outside both organizations. The Free Officers had their own publications which were printed secretly by the DMNL and either distributed by the Free Officers or posted by the mail. Because it was too dangerous for the Free Officers to write, print, and distribute their leaflets, they handed some of that responsibility to their communist allies.[15]

Nasser himself was a main actor in this scheme. It has been said that at that time he owned a black Citroen which he used to drive to a place near Roda on the Nile, where, as a Free Officer representative, he would wait for his DMNL contact to appear. The contact was responsible for making the connection between the DMNL's central committee, its printing apparatus, and the Free Officers' representative. That middleman, Milko Milkonian, was an Armenian electrical engineer who owned a shop for repairing radios. His job within the DMNL was to take packets from the printing department and deliver them to the man in the black Citroen who was called "Maurice." Milkonian did not know the contents of the packages nor the identity of his contact until after the 1952 revolution when Milkonian along with the whole of the DMNL's printing department was arrested by Nasser, then a leader of the Revolutionary Command Council.[16] This was Nasser's abrupt way of saying that the symbiotic relationship between the Free Officers and the communists was over. It demonstrated to the left that the Free Officers' organization was fearful of the communists and was perhaps even being pressured by the religious, nationalist, and anticommunist elements within the group. The communists could no longer look forward to a mutually friendly relationship with Egypt's new power brokers.

Although the association between the DMNL and the Free Officers was somewhat irregular just after the coup because of the un-

timely labor strike at Kafr al-Dawwar, six months later the party became disenchanted with the direction of military rule and criticized
it as conforming to the interests of the national bourgeoisie. Despite
the fact that the King was expelled and the backs of the feudalists
were broken by Nasser's land reform, the Officers disappointed the
left when they signed an accord on the Sudan considered by the communists to be unfavorable to Egypt, accepted an unpopular military
alliance with Great Britain, and imprisoned Egyptian nationalists. The
DMNL announced that the Officers had ceded to the pressures of imperialism and were no longer allies.[17]

Other wings of the communist movement provided differing
analyses of the military movement. The ECP opposed the military
rulers after their first or second week in power and called the coup
a military dictatorship with some fascist coloring.[18] Ismail Sabri Abd
Allah remarked:

> We were confused first because of two contradicting things. We
> thought that objectively the overthrow of the King was some-
> thing very positive but due to our political education we believed
> that nothing good and durable could come from the army. The
> army was a tool of oppression, conservative by definition, and to
> us there was nothing that could be called a progressive coup d'etat.
> We were against coups. We were for revolution. In the first days
> our position was ambiguous, saluting the overthrow of the King
> but asking the military to fraternize with the population and
> form neighborhood committees and village committees of work-
> ers and soldiers. . . . Then there was a strike at Kafr al-Dawwar.
> The army intervened and two leaders of the strike were hanged.
> Then we said that this is a fascist regime.[19]

The ECP took, perhaps, the most critical line of all the other
underground groups against the revolution and refused entirely to
cooperate with the officers. Even the reformist laws — land reform and
the declaration of the republic in particular—went unpraised by the
members of the ECP.

The New Regime of the Free Officers

Although a variety of views and sentiments prevailed within the Free
Officers Movement, the Officers first joined together primarily on the
basis of a collective understanding of the problems enfeebling Egyp-

tian society, namely the British occupation and economic backwardness. Once in power, their chief tasks centered on achieving national liberation and fostering economic development. As Maxime Rodinson noted, the democratizing of Egypt's economic and social life figured into the Free Officers' program mainly as a corollary of their other overriding aim which was to establish a strong and independent nation.[20]

The Free Officers had only the vaguest ideas about the reorganization and revitalization of society and they lacked a concrete political program which could have helped direct them toward the realization of their nationalist aspirations. From July 1952 until March 1954, Egypt's general political situation was in flux and rivalry developed inside the leadership of the revolution. Although the Free Officers, (renamed the Revolutionary Command Council after the coup, RCC), exercised effective power through their domination of every essential army unit, early on they needed to legitimize their authority in society. This was accomplished through the appointment of well known and popular national figures to leadership positions: General Muhammad Naguib, a prominent nationalist hero, was given the presidency of the RCC; and Ali Mahir, who, although a political chameleon was known as an anti-British politician, was asked to lead the Cabinet.

From the outset there were two centers of power. There was the army, ostensibly headed by Naguib which set policy, and there was the government headed by civilians exercising in principle executive power. Since King Faruq had been exiled on July 26, 1952, royal authority could no longer intervene in Egyptian political and social affairs. But Egyptian politics proved more complex than the machinations of the King himself and it did not take long before the RCC was awakened to the realities of a complicated political situation. Pressure groups, organized political parties, and articulate representatives of the privileged classes began trying to influence the direction of politics. Each tried to secure a spokesman for various claims and interests. The multiplicity of opinions which existed and the absence of a homogeneous national outlook were considered by the RCC damaging to national unity and detrimental to the survival of the revolution. From the start, pluralist trends were neither accepted nor tolerated and the RCC dealt harshly with divergent challenges in order to consolidate its authority.

The first jolt suffered by the Officers came on August 12, only weeks after their accession to power. It was this early in the new regime's life that its attitude to the popular masses was indelibly, if

cruelly, illustrated to the nation at large. The revealing incident occurred at Kafr al-Dawwar and it marked the first signs of communist
disenchantment with military policy.

Kafr al-Dawwar was located thirty kilometers from Alexandria,
a small industrial area, made up of two large textile factories owned
by the Misr Fine Spinning and Weaving Company and the Sabahi al-
Bayda Company, plus a workers' housing complex. By the end of the
1940s, there were some ten thousand workers in the Misr Fine Spinning and Weaving Company and the average wage of the workers was
about 17 piasters a day, low even by the standards of the time. The
workers, whose preoccupation with the problems of housing, health
care, and the treatment they received by the bosses predated the revolution, were jubilant with the revolutionary slogans raised by the RCC.
Because they considered the political climate favorable to their interests, the workers in the company plant struck on August 12, 1952,
for improved conditions: higher wages, increased annual leave with
pay, recognition of the union, and the dismissal of two members on
the managerial staff.

These labor grievances were not new. The workers had alerted
the company to their dissatisfaction when they forwarded their demands to the company's administration several months before the
power change. Their appeal at that time, however, was not addressed
by the company. After the accession to power of the Free Officers and
subsequent to the successful negotiations at the neighboring Sabahi
al-Bayda Company, the workers at Misr believed they needed to wait
no longer. Presuming that both right and authority were on their side,
they moved. In retrospect, Hilmi Yassin commented:

> It was very natural that the workers should start a movement in
> Kafr al-Dawwar because they heard the communiques of the revo-
> lution which announced that the kingdom was abolished, that
> the regime was against injustice, that the rights of the people would
> be restored. It was natural that workers who had been oppressed
> for a very long time, would put forward their demands. . . . The
> management of the company represented elements of the old re-
> gime. They were capitalists, very reactionary . . . and against both
> the workers and the revolution.[21]

Workers' hopes and expectations, however, were quickly shattered by
the reality of a harsh, uncompromising military rule. Muhammad
Mitwali al-Shaarawi present at the strike recalled the details:

Between August tenth and thirteenth, there was enthusiasm and zeal among the workers. Discussions spread and a movement for a strike at Misr was underway. . . . But there were two trends among the workers; one demanded a speedy strike to catch up with the workers of al-Bayda and to reach the same result; the other wanted to follow a legal path and in accordance with Law #85 of 1945 inform the company of the intentions to strike at least fifteen days before its outbreak. . . . I met with some of the workers from all the sections of the factory and we decided to follow a legal path. . . . We went to the company administration with our determination to strike, presented our demands and gave management fifteen days to negotiate. . . . The same evening [August 12] a few of us were called to the home of Ali Suwaylim where he announced that the strike would proceed on that night. Discussion ensued but we realized that we were called to his house to be informed that the strike had begun.[22]

Those who supported the legal path did not prevail and the workers were immediately called out to protest their condition. At about 7:00 p.m. on August 12, the workers assembled in front of the plant and perhaps naively asked for the redress of their grievances "in the name of Muhammad Naguib and the revolution."[23] The company refused the requests categorically and by 9:30 p.m. had called in the head of the police of Kafr al-Dawwar, Numan al-Ashmawi, to disperse the crowd. The police, using force, blockaded some of the striking workers inside the factory. Other workers outside defended themselves against the authorities by throwing rocks. The collision between the workers and the police left one worker dead and many from both sides wounded.[24] During the fracas, two office buildings were set on fire. It remains unclear who was responsible for the destruction.

The situation was further complicated when Numan al-Ashmawi notified the leadership of the army in Alexandria that the workers had struck and were destroying the factory. Five hundred soldiers and officers arrived at 3:00 a.m. and surrounded the factory preventing anyone from leaving or entering the building. Khalid Muhyi al-Din remembered that night:

I was at the cavalry barracks. They woke me up and told me that there was a demonstration at Kafr al-Dawwar and that the workers burned the factory. . . . I was at the time the Intelligence Officer in the cavalry and a member of the Revolutionary Council. . . . I

woke al-Shafii and he gave orders to the battalion and they went.
. . . The army entered Kafr al-Dawwar, surrounded the fire and put
it out. Then they asked for the names of the workers involved.
Some witnesses gave names. There were arrests.[25]

A clash with the army did ensue but afterward those workers blockaded inside the factory were allowed to leave.

Meanwhile, the government had issued a statement about the
turmoil in which it stated that the new nationalist government was
earnest in its goals of rescuing the society from confusion, imposing
justice, and improving the standard of living of the poor. It announced
that the problems of workers, their rights, and their concern for the
well-being of their children and families were among the government's
primary interests. But it stressed it would not hesitate to seize agitators, arrest strikers, and put them before the military tribunal to
be tried for treasonous crimes which sabotage the national interest.[26]
All workers were put on notice by the government to moderate their
actions and demands.

The next morning, August 13, a demonstration was underway,
starting from the housing area of the community and moving toward
the factory, it included between five hundred and one thousand workers. (See Figure 5.) At its head was Mustafa Khamis, an active trade
unionist and communist sympathizer. The workers shouted nationalist and revolutionary slogans and called for the release of the workers who had been arrested. This was a peaceful march and there were
no clashes between the demonstrators and the troops.

At the same time a second demonstration was undertaken following a different path—from the workers' houses to al-Mahmudiyya
Canal. This procession included some one thousand to two thousand
workers. Again, revolutionary chants were heard. At some point a
pitched battle between the workers and soldiers broke out, the result
of which was the death of a number of workers and two soldiers. The
conflict stirred up considerable emotion and caused no small measure of resentment. Al-Shaarawi continued:

When the first demonstration of Mustafa Khamis was marching
past the factory, one Aziz al-Jamal, nephew of Husayn al-Jamal,
General Director of the Misr Company, fired some shots. At that
point, the soldiers thought that the demonstration was armed.
. . . The forces sent shots into the air, not hitting anyone and dis-

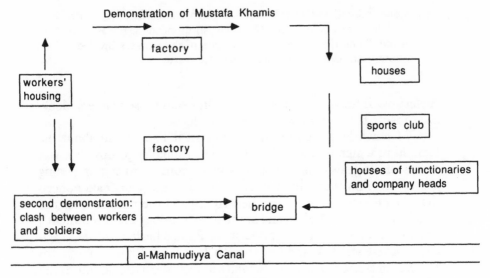

Figure 5
The Village of Kafr Al-Dawwar, August 13, 1952

persing the crowd. Meanwhile, Mustafa Khamis tried to pass over the bridge in order to lead his group behind the second line of demonstrators. Mistakenly, he was later blamed for the killing of the soldiers despite the fact that his demonstration . . . had no connection with the place in which the soldiers were killed. He came from the housing area whereas the other demonstration passed by al-Mahmudiyya Canal.[27]

There are a host of questions about the incident at Kafr al-Dawwar which remain unanswered. Who actually called the strike and who decided not to pursue legal channels? Who started the fire at the factory and why? Why did Aziz al-Jamal fire shots into the demonstration? Did the plant administration instigate the trouble to drive a wedge between the workers and the revolution?

Although the precise history of the events at Kafr al-Dawwar has never been disentangled, one fact has been established by Marie Dominique Gresh: Hafiz al-Afifi, past chief of the Royal Cabinet and well known Anglophile, was present on the night of the strike. According to Gresh, he gave as the reason for his visit the need to confer with the company's management. Afterward, there were many who questioned the validity of this statement and doubted his benevolence for the new regime. They suspected him of complicity with the company's efforts to crush working class militancy and assumed he was at the factory to stir up unrest.[28]

Members of the left speculated that the company administration provoked the strike to force the RCC to punish the workers, which, in turn, would cause labor militants to break with the new government. The company's intent, they believed, was to weaken the military leadership and alienate its following.

Although the behavior of the company officials remains unexplained, the actions of the RCC are well documented. On August 14, a hastily convened summary court martial was appointed to try the alleged leaders of the strike among whom were Mustafa Khamis and Ahmad al-Bakri. Presiding over the military court was one of the Free Officers, Abd al-Munim Amin who, according to Khalid Muhyi al-Din, was chosen because he was part of the RCC and one of the links with the American Embassy. Since the Council wanted to establish good relations with the United States, still considered a friendly super power, he was a prime choice.[29]

On August 18 the sentences were passed: Mustafa Khamis and Ahmad al-Bakri were condemned to death by hanging, guilty of "a grave crime against the state." Six others were given sentences of ten to fifteen years hard labor; five were sentenced to five to eight years; three were condemned to one to three years. The hangings were performed on the factory grounds. If nothing else was clear, the RCC wanted to make an example of anyone who threatened the stability of the new regime. A message was sent to the working class: no independent mass initiatives would be tolerated. Moreover, the direction of the Council was established: it was nationalist in orientation without being popularist and without relying on the support of the masses. Khalid Muhyi al-Din was present during the deliberations of the RCC and he remarked:

> The military court gave Khamis and Bakri the death penalty but there was resistance in the Council to this. I remember Gamal Abdul Nasser . . . and I think Yusuf Siddiq, although I am not sure about him . . . were against the decision. The majority were in favor. We tried to postpone it, we tried to have a judgment other than the death penalty . . . but the Council wanted to make the workers and the people afraid of any activity that sabotaged the government. . . . They said "if we let workers strike and burn fac-

tories we will not be able to control them. So we must treat them
like soldiers and make them afraid." Also, they were afraid of the
workers, and at this time there was the Soviet Union and communism. In the back of their minds they were afraid of this. . . .
It was a tragedy.[30]

Ahmad al-Bakri was a humble worker who was inspired by the
revolution to participate in trade union activities. The background
of Khamis is more difficult to determine. Although it has been claimed
that he was a member of the ECP[31] and of a small group called the
Red Star Organization,[32] conclusive evidence is hard to find. What
appears accurate is that Khamis was a progressive minded trade unionist who might have been a friend of the communist movement. The
judgment of posterity is that he and al-Bakri were unfairly accused
and tragically hanged.

Another question raised in the context of the Kafr al-Dawwar
episode is the conduct of the DMNL. While other communist groups
immediately condemned the military's shockingly extreme behavior,
the DMNL acted more cautiously. Representatives of the Preparatory
Committee to Establish a General Trade Union Federation, which was
led by the DMNL, went to Kafr al-Dawwar to counsel the workers.
Ahmad Taha and Abd al-Munim al-Ghazzali, representatives of the
Committee, explained to the workers that there should be collaboration between them and the army movement. They suggested that the
labor movement was being sabotaged by the enemies of the revolution and by adversaries of the working class.[33] The Committee distributed a statement against the strike and in favor of a negotiated
settlement with the company.[34]

The DMNL was, in fact, against any move that would provide
the RCC the occasion to be harsh with the workers. Suspecting that
the strike, the fire, the clashes with the army and the police were in-
stigated by the factory management, they tried to convince the workers that any division between them and the military regime would
be detrimental to the national movement. Ahmad Taha stated em-
phatically that "some people who were connected with the owners
of the factory, and especially Hafiz al-Afifi, engineered this strike."[35]
Despite the words of caution preached by the Committee and the
DMNL, events moved very quickly and in the end, the DMNL had
little impact on the situation. All it could do was to condemn the
hanging of the workers Khamis and al-Bakri and criticize the military's inflexible behavior. Although the DMNL felt betrayed by the

RCC's harsh actions at Kafr al-Dawwar, the organization did not break with the Free Officers until January 1953 when political parties were abolished and the complexion of the military regime became even clearer.

On September 7, 1952, the second major political crisis for the RCC materialized when the inherently ambiguous relationship between the RCC and the civilian Cabinet of Ali Mahir produced an unavoidable power struggle which led to Mahir's resignation. The specific issue of contention at the time was the agrarian reform law, one of the earliest symbols of Free Officer policy, and one that Ali Mahir fundamentally disagreed with and refused to support. Promulgated on September 9, the law called for the limitation of ownership of up to two hundred *faddans* of land with the provision that a family with two or more children could retain an additional one hundred *faddans.* Every owner was to be indemnified in negotiable government bonds and the government was to be the sole distributor of expropriated land. The plan, which was designed by Ahmad Fuad and Rashid al-Barawi, both Marxist economists, succeeded in fragmenting the social, political, and economic power of the large landlords. The DMNL, at the time, applauded the program of land redistribution and in general believed that the officers were moving in a forward looking direction thanks to the advice of Marxists within the RCC. In contrast, Ali Mahir considered this new law a radical and destructive piece of legislation and preferred resignation to complicity.

With little internal dislocation, President Naguib assumed Ali Mahir's responsibilities with the effect that the army was slowly institutionalizing itself and becoming involved in all aspects of day to day political life. Civilian politicians were increasingly relegated to posts of only cosmetic importance as the military vanguard emerged from behind the scenes to take charge of national affairs.

The Struggle for Power

After the removal of the royal family, the expropriation of the landlords and pashas, the silencing of the political parties, and the show of force against the working class, the RCC was the principal political power in the country. Especially after Muhammad Naguib emerged as president of the government and the civilian ministers began receiving orders from the military, it became clear that the RCC had decided to take hold of exclusive authority in the country. In consequence, all political forces once active in royalist Egypt stepped up their agitation and pressure tactics within and outside the army in a determined effort to maintain the pluralist society. From the vantage point of the Wafd, the Muslim Brotherhood, and the communists, it was essential that political freedom be retained.

The Free Officers felt uncertain in their new roles as leaders of Egypt; they feared competition, resented criticism, and rejected any form of opposition. But their insecurity was short-lived. For though they might have initially supported the idea of returning political power to a civilian leadership and advocated representative parliamentary institutions, once their authority solidified, their views changed. As time passed, the military clique began feeling comfortable in their positions. Not only did they delight in ruling but they believed they had a mission to accomplish. Unlike the political parties of the past, which they judged to be corrupt, antidemocratic, and unrepresentative of the will of the people, the junta came to believe that the independence and modernization of Egypt could only be achieved by a military leadership. In the view of the Free Officers, a democratically elected parliament composed of diverse and often conflicting opinions was simply unsuitable to the needs of the day.[36]

On January 16, 1953, the RCC dissolved all political parties except the Muslim Brotherhood.[37] One week later, the government created Liberation Rally, a party designed to express the opinions of the military, fill the gap between the regime and the masses, and subtly contain political unrest.[38] Further revealing the political inclinations of the RCC, the government began to clamp down on independent sources of activity: for example, communists were arrested and imprisoned, opposition newspapers such as *al-Katib* (The Scribe) and *al-Muarada* (The Opposition) were dissolved, and members of the Peace Movement were harassed.

Such constraint smothered civilian political activity and obstructed the path to a democratic Egypt. Striking back, the communists, and in particular, members of the DMNL, the ECP, and the Organization of Popular Democracy, joined with members of the left-wing Wafd, several members of the Muslim Brotherhood, the Peace Movement, the Socialist Party, and some independent workers and intellectuals to form the United Revolutionary Front in February 1953 in Alexandria. In April 1953 a branch was established in Cairo and it was renamed the National Democratic Front.[39]

According to the radical opposition, since no single group was capable of rising up against military authoritarianism and challenging its political control over society, a union of diverse forces was needed to disable the military government. Within the structure of a "front," dissidents agitated for the return of constitutional life and the restoration of the fundamental liberties of democracy. The front's main objective was to end military dictatorship, reestablish political and civil rights, and completely liberate the country from the lingering hold of colonialism.[40]

The National Democratic Front was precisely the type of activity the communists wanted to engage in. It brought the left out of its chronic isolation, it offered a measure of respectability, and it provided a legitimate platform from which to speak. It also had the potential of facilitating the gradual infiltration of rival parties.

Specifically, members of the DMNL approached selected Wafdists and suggested the idea of united activity after the military had confiscated the communist publications *al-Wajib, al-Katib,* and *al-Malayin.* Although the Wafd was reluctant at first to join the front, perhaps questioning the reliability of the communists and the political wisdom of allying with them, it was always open to negotiations with the left. When the DMNL was first rebuffed, the organization's representatives began talking to rank and file Wafdists aiming at attracting the base of the Wafd and, especially, the heads of the youth committees in the neighborhoods. It was successful in recruiting some Wafdist youth who began pressuring the mainstream of the party to associate with the communists. With the simultaneous issuance of the military law prohibiting political parties and the arrest of some Wafdist sympathizers, coordination was expedited and the Wafd agreed to the union. Yusuf Hilmi, head of the Peace Movement in Egypt, and on close terms with both groups, mediated the merger. Later, others of different political persuasions, as well, were recruited by the front on an individual basis.[41]

Muhammad Fuad Munir, active in the DMNL, presented the following testimony about the front before a military court while being tried for subversive activities:

> When I came to be responsible for the Alexandria area [of the DMNL] in February 1953, there were contacts between the DMNL and Wafdist youth about establishing a front in Alexandria, before the main front was to be founded in Cairo. The contacts resulted in the founding of the United Revolutionary Front. Its purpose was to demand the end of martial law, to demand democratic

freedoms, to insist that Egypt not enter into colonial alliances, and to guide people toward armed struggle against the British.[42]

In Alexandria, the front concentrated on outreach—on circulating its views to as wide an audience as possible. A number of publications were issued among which were the group's program, a pamphlet condemning the dissolution of political parties, and a statement critiquing the economic conditions in Egypt targeting in particular the reductions in salaries, decreases in bread size, hikes in sugar prices, and increases in tram fares as the most injurious to the popular classes. The group also organized a demonstration at the College of Law at Alexandria University to protest the visit of Gamal Abdul Nasser to the city.[43]

Although the groundwork for the front was laid in Alexandria, its central office was set up in Cairo in April 1953 with Zaki Murad representing the DMNL and the Peace Movement, and Ibrahim Faraj and Hanafi Sharif speaking in behalf of the Wafd. In Cairo, the members decided to change the group's name to the National Democratic Front. The Cairo branch was responsible for launching the front's organ, al-Jabha (The Front). In its first issue on June 12, 1953, it identified three primary goals: to expel Anglo-American imperialism and all occupation forces; to achieve political and economic democracy; and to offer solidarity to other peoples of the world in order to prevent war and establish peace.[44] It stated further that:

> The achievement of these goals cannot be implemented except through the overthrow of the fascist military rule. The purpose of the front is to unify and coordinate all the nationalist forces in the sacred battle for independence and democracy.[45]

The front's continued denunciations of military rule did not escape the attention of the authorities. In November of 1953 about forty members of the group were arrested as the military government's campaign to emasculate its opposition escalated.

Imprisoning leaders of the opposition did temporarily weaken the protest against the antidemocratic trend of the military officers. However, it also deepened the divisions within the RCC itself. Muhammad Naguib, in theory the leader of the government, was unequivocally committed to the return of constitutional life. He was increasingly troubled by the authoritarian dispositions of his colleagues and their refusal to entertain his suggestions for liberalization and reform. Naguib supported the founding of a parliamentary republic which would guarantee personal and political freedoms and temper the restrictions imposed by a military junta. Nasser, who opposed the relinquishment of authority and worried about both underground and legal opposition, also became apprehensive about Naguib's national popularity. This was mainly because Naguib was being praised by the nation for the positive developments of the revolution while Nasser was in fact its unrecognized architect.

Like Naguib, Khalid Muhyi al-Din was disenchanted with the antidemocratic actions of the military government. Of the RCC he said:

> We agreed that if the army came to power we would open the door for a real democratic state. There would be constitutional life and elections. . . . I wanted legality, a multi-party system . . . and I knew that under the military, the left would have no room. So the quick return to democratic life was in my interests. . . .
>
> It was in this period that I began wanting to leave the Council . . . but Abdul Nasser counselled me against this . . . [saying] "you may stop us from going too far to the right."[46]

While Nasser wanted to tighten his grasp over the regime, Naguib hoped to preside over its demise and the transition back to parliamentary life. The situation finally became intolerable for Nasser and it was only a matter of time before the growing disenchantment turned into open conflict. Naguib was the symbol of the revolution, but he had no roots in the original Free Officers Movement. Nasser was the real power behind the scenes. In January 1954 after the occurrence of anti-Nasser demonstrations at Cairo University, Nasser unilaterally outlawed the Muslim Brotherhood in response to its antagonistic behavior. He did not consult Naguib about his intentions.[47] The conflict between Naguib and Nasser finally occurred on February 24 when Naguib openly criticized the regime for its repressive measures and demanded a "right of veto" over the Council's decisions. Nasser and his supporters were stunned by Naguib's outburst and by the tender of his resignation which followed. After a meeting of the Council took place, the following statement was issued:

> In spite of the shock that this news will give to public opinion, we have had to break with Naguib who aimed at dictatorship, criticized in public and to foreigners decisions that had been made by a majority, and with no thought but his own popularity, played a double game by coming to an understanding with the opposition.[48]

Chided for selfishly trying to seize power and disrupting the co-operation between members of the government, Naguib's resignation as president, prime minister, and chairman of the RCC was accepted. Nasser was proclaimed chairman of the Council and prime minister; the presidency of the Republic remained vacant. These political changes sent shock waves through the country, and people mourned Naguib's departure. Even within the military, dissension spread. Few were unaware that the "smiling General [Naguib]" was a symbol of the unity between the different tendencies in the army, between the army and the country, and between Egypt and the Sudan.[49] Khalid Muhyi al-Din confirmed this:

> Naguib was the symbol of the revolution and he began to gain the sympathy of the people and he began to realize that although his strength within the Free Officers was not so strong, his national popularity was great. Abdul Nasser realized he was becoming too dangerous and wanted to control him. Naguib refused. A struggle started . . . over constitutional life and when the crisis came to an end Naguib resigned and the situation exploded. We had built a hero and then suddenly we said to the people, "your hero is bad." This was a miscalculation by Abdul Nasser.[50]

The liberal and progressive factions in the army, led by Khalid Muhyi al-Din's cavalry officers, challenged Nasser in an effort to reinstate Naguib in office. Muhyi al-Din continued:

> After Naguib's resignation, the country exploded against the Revolutionary Council. Part of the explosion was in the cavalry corps. We called a meeting and asked Nasser to come. I had initially refused to accept the resignation of Naguib in the Council but Nasser said that we must accept the resignation unanimously. I said, "All right, but after a week I will resign . . . because I don't agree with this policy. . . ." The next day the cavalry corps called

a meeting first with Husayn al-Shafii . . . and later with Gamal Abdul Nasser and they said of Naguib, "We are his men, make him President of the Republic, otherwise you can not depend on the cavalry. This is for the interest of Egypt and the Sudan. The people want a constitution." Nasser felt that the people were against him and the cavalry was against him and he felt a break-down. He called me and said, "Nobody can cooperate with Naguib except you. . . . So before dawn we must go to Naguib and tell him he is accepted as President of the Republic. . . ." In the morn-ing I went to Naguib and he agreed. . . . When I came back from Naguib's house, the artillery and infantry were surrounding the cavalry. The air force was present. I was arrested.[51]

Khalid Muhyi al-Din was made to pay for his support of Naguib. But his arrest did not temper the population's joy after learning of Naguib's reinstatement.

In January 1954 it had seemed that most segments of the coun-try were against Nasser—Naguib had supporters among the people, parts of the army, the Wafd, the communist movement, the Muslim Brotherhood, and the upper classes. Yet, despite long odds against him, Nasser was to emerge from his conflict with Naguib, (and through him with constitutionalism), victorious. Nasser's tactical genius served his cause well: he made concessions to the people, convinced the army of his indispensability and so won back its confidence, and forced Naguib to make mistakes which isolated him from his supporters.

In early March, as a stopgap, Nasser promised the convocation of a Constituent Assembly to be held in July. Furthermore, he lifted censorship and freed a number of political prisoners from jail. When Naguib was reinstated on March 8 as prime minister and chairman of the RCC, Nasser took over his old post as deputy prime minister. Then on March 24, Nasser announced that come July 24, "the revolu-tion would be considered over." Contrary to expectations, this was not the beginning of a program of conciliation. Rather, Abdul Nasser was engaging in a calculated subterfuge designed to deceive and weaken Naguib.

Within a few weeks, Nasser united the army around himself by pointing out what it would lose if the military forfeited control. He stigmatized and isolated Khalid Muhyi al-Din and the pluralists, all the while emphasizing Naguib's questionable compromises with the old guard politicians. Nasser staged strikes and demonstrations under the auspices of Liberation Rally on March 25, 26, and 27, in Cairo and Alexandria in support of his own leadership and in opposition to the return of democratic life. This made it possible for the regime to withdraw from its promises to restore parliamentarianism and liberalism. On March 29, the RCC announced the postponement of the implementation of the March resolutions until January 1956. Naguib was again ousted from the government and from the RCC, and on April 5, a series of measures were instituted which were designed to strengthen the RCC's position and "protect the revolution."

In the very short span of one month, then, Naguib's position was dramatically weakened. Naguib's personal efforts to revive parliamentarianism and the propaganda drummed up by Nasser led segments of the army and the population to believe that Naguib would return Egypt to its prerevolutionary political status, which meant massive inequality, unchecked elitism, and widespread corruption. Naguib was thought to be too close to leaders of the Wafd, and his victory, it was feared, would return the discredited Wafd to power. Because Nasser convinced many that pluralism was nothing more than a disguise for the kind of regime which had presided over Egypt's suffering and humiliation in the past, Naguib was denounced. Khalid Muhyi al-Din concluded that:

> The movement of 1954 failed because people were not ready to come back to the old political system. They were not in favor of real democratic life. They wanted a strong leader to reform the country. Their slogan was "Egypt is in need of a just dictator. . . ." The democratic trend was found only among lawyers, students and some part of the working class. But the majority of people were in favor of keeping the situation as it was because there was a probability of reform. So the *coup* of Nasser's succeeded. . . . The population was fed up with the old system and it thought that the mistakes of the past came directly from the multi-party system.[52]

The struggle of February-March 1954 was part of an ideological and political battle waged to determine how the revolution would proceed. Effectively, the issue at hand was, how and by whom should the country be run? Nasser not only knew in what direction he wanted Egypt to move, but he was also shrewd in his dealings with his rivals, weakening them by stressing Egypt's need for a new plan to win independence and to assure modernization. During the "liberal age" in Egypt, when parliamentary government prevailed and some degree of freedom was afforded its citizens, too little was achieved to convince the population of democracy's advantages.

By March 1954 the internal political struggle came to an end and authoritarianism returned again to Egypt. Demonstrations by the Muslim Brotherhood, the Wafd, and the communists were put down. Universities were closed. By April 18 Nasser was the undisputed leader of the revolution and the top political figure in the country. With Nasser's victory, the fate of the Marxists in the RCC and in the country was sealed: Khalid Muhyi al-Din was expelled from Egypt and exiled temporarily to Europe; Yusuf Siddiq had withdrawn from Nasser's circle; and the arrest and prosecution of communists were stepped up with dozens of people receiving long-term jail sentences at hard labor. If there had ever been a "honeymoon" period granted by the military regime to the communists, it was officially over by this time.

Communist Accommodation with the Government

The Marxist left, though not very powerful or supported by the masses, nonetheless represented one of the elements in the political struggle in the immediate postrevolutionary period. As such, each of the three most significant communist organizations in Egypt, the DMNL, the ECP, and the Workers' Vanguard made evaluations of the new regime which reflected their separate ideologies and their relationship to the power brokers.

The DMNL supported the military government because in many ways it was linked to it. There were connections which dated back to 1950, and some of the communists close to Nasser contributed to the Six Principles published soon after the change of power. When Nasser worked with the DMNL, it was because he needed its support in the critical period just before the revolution. Yet, in the years between 1952 and 1954, when he was struggling to maintain his power against a range of center-right forces including the old feudalists, members of the established political parties, and the state apparatus, he no longer seemed to need his communist associates.

Almost from the start, the Egyptian Communist Party was vitriolic in its denunciation of the events of July 23. The party condemned the regime's takeover as a military coup d'etat with fascist tendencies, and its members distributed tracts labeling Nasser a traitor and dictator.

A middle position was taken by the Workers' Vanguard Party, led by Ahmad Sadiq Saad, Raymond Duwayk, Abu Sayf Yusuf, and Yusuf Darwish. This group adopted a pragmatic attitude which backed the Free Officers Movement in its struggle against the British occupation and the Palace, but was quietly critical of the regime's inability to tolerate pluralism in the political arena.

The rapid pace of events soon brought the communist movement temporarily together. First, all the Marxist groups condemned the hanging of the two workers at Kafr al-Dawwar. Although the DMNL counseled the trade unionists not to antagonize the new government, even this traditionally supportive group was forced to pull back in its accommodation with the regime. Second, when Nasser signed the evacuation treaty with Great Britain in October 1954, the communists found additional reasons militating toward opposition to the revolution. Because the agreement allowed for the reoccupation of Egypt by British troops or their allies in the event or threat of war, the left rejected the settlement and persisted in attacking the regime, to different degrees, until 1955. In April of that year, Nasser went to the Bandung Conference and emerged with Tito and Nehru as leaders of the movement of positive neutralism. In September, he signed the arms deal with Czechoslovakia by which he established a military and political relationship with the Soviet Union. From that time, all communists adopted a positive assessment of the regime, and the government was applauded for its anticolonialist, anti-imperialist, and antifeudalist policies. When Nasser nationalized the Suez Canal Company in July 1956, the Marxists felt vindicated, as if given the necessary proof that their backing was well deserved. They remained critical only of the antidemocratic nature of the government.

When the political situation became tense as a result of the attack against Egypt by Israel, Britain, and France in October 1956, a significant segment of the country came to the service of the regime. Although the more conservative elements in Egypt recommended surrendering to the tripartite forces, the communists joined the popular resistance against the attackers and were important actors in the armed struggle against colonialist intervention. The left was now advocating and acting upon the united front strategy against imperialism which was initially put forward by Henri Curiel in the 1940s.

After the evacuation of Port Said, an unspoken, unofficial alliance between the regime and the communists took effect. At this time, Nasser was emerging as the leader of the Arab world and spokesman for Third World independence and development. He was enjoying the fact that he had nationalized the Suez Canal Company and got away with it, and that he had repelled the tripartite aggressors.[53] Because Nasser intended to restructure the country after the departure of the foreign forces, he needed the support of those committed to national independence and social change.[54] While he formally refused to allow the communists to organize legally and to build up their strength through open political activity, as a practical matter he took a fairly conciliatory stand toward them: communists were not imprisoned between 1956 and the end of 1958, left-wing publishing houses flourished, and the daily newspaper *al-Masa,* headed by Khalid Muhyi al-Din, operated quite successfully. This was a period of accommodation with the communists, but Nasser always kept his distance from the left.

After Suez, many of the communists were questioning why a total unification of the Marxist movement had not occurred. Some argued that since it was possible for the left to move closer to the petty-bourgeois military officers through the common front against colonialism in 1956, then there was no justification for the leftist organizations not to move closer to each other. It was considered aberrational that Marxists stood close to the vanguard of the revolution and yet stood in conflict with themselves. This was a very compelling argument in favor of the unity of the communist movement.

Due to the semi-open status which the communist movement enjoyed, Marxists were able to talk to one another and to draw closer together. In November 1957, the DMNL, and factions which had temporarily split from it, joined with the ECP to form the Unified Egyptian Communist Party. When the Workers' Vanguard entered the party on January 8, 1958, it was renamed the United Communist Party of Egypt. The entire Marxist movement had now come together. Momentary elation spread through the communist movement, but cause for celebration was short-lived.

Like other attempts to unify the communist groups, this effort ended in failure; after some six months, a faction originally from the DMNL withdrew from the party. A basic problem with this union was that although lengthy discussions among the leaderships did take place, those in control did not probe deeply enough into the differences which, in reality, divided the organizations since times past. They did not take into account the real personal enmities among the leaders and also the class character and practical experience of the separate groups. From the start, there was a jockeying for positions which led to vindictive quarrels, or compromises which caused dissension. In the end, there was no sincere conviction that this super-ficial unity should continue. When disagreements arose and could not be easily resolved, the tendency to abandon common principles and revert back to individual organizations resurfaced.[55]

Soon after unification, the communists were required to make difficult decisions regarding Egypt's role in Arab affairs. With new regional politics emerging and dramatic changes taking place, the communists were compelled to take a stand. In February 1958, Syria and Egypt merged and the United Arab Republic was formed. All po-litical parties in Syria were disbanded, including the Communist Party led by Khalid Bakdash, according to Nasser's principle of one party rule. The Syrian communists resisted the dissolution of their party and advocated a type of federation between Egypt and Syria rather than total integration. This, of course, would have allowed for the continuation of the multi-party system in Syria in which Bakdash and his followers were important actors. But since both the Nasserists and the Bathists in Damascus wanted the liquidation of the communists, they opposed Bakdash and ousted him from Syria.

The newly formed United Communist Party of Egypt debated the issue of Arab unity on its own terms, and on the narrower basis of how it would affect the communists directly. The party accepted the predominant theory in the contemporary Arab national movement that unification of the peoples of a region based on common language, history, and culture was advantageous. It pointed to the benefits of joint economic and political activity in resisting western imperial-ism and Zionist expansionism. But, while the party did adopt a posi-tive consensus on the principle of unity, there was disagreement con-cerning the type of merger which should take place. In keeping with its historic sympathies, a DMNL contingent argued strongly for agree-ment with the government's position; other members opposed this on the basis of solidarity with a sister Arab communist party. In the end, Khalid Bakdash's position was followed, which resulted in divi-sion within the Egyptian communist movement.

While the United Communist Party of Egypt survived the inter-nal debates on the issue of Syrian-Egyptian unification, it did not outlive the dissension caused by the Iraqi revolution of July 1958. When Abd al-Karim Qassim emerged as the leader of the new revolution he rejected the proposed alliance with the U.A.R. because, in his view, pan-Arabism as led by Nasser could only lead to Iraq's subordination to a leadership in Cairo. Qassim's main interests were to safeguard his country's independence and to protect his own position. In his struggle against Nasser and pan-Arab nationalism, Qassim allied with the Iraqi communists who had been playing a significant role in the political affairs of the country and had learned an important lesson from the Syrian experience during unity.

The United Communist Party of Egypt, which had a preexisting relationship with the Iraqi left, was encouraged by it to oppose Nasser's efforts to export pan-Arabism to Baghdad. When this issue was debated in the party intense disagreement broke down the last semblance of organizational harmony. Unity was sacrificed after the majority decided to adopt a pro-Qassim stand and members of the DMNL faction withdrew in protest. Ultimately, the unification of Egyptian communists proved premature and unable to withstand ideological division. Because Nasser feared that Qassim and the Iraqi communists posed a serious threat to his leadership in the Arab world, he deeply resented the United Communist Party of Egypt's disloyalty to him. As a result, the accommodating relationship between Nasser and the Egyptian communists ended.

In essence, because the historic enmities which had separated the groups during the Second World War had not been resolved, in the 1950s the party perpetuated the tradition of factionalism and continued to contain within itself the seeds of division. Isolated from mainstream society, absent from the trade union movement, and generally unable to find an independent platform which could compete with Nasser's successful championing of the causes of Arab nationalism and antiimperialism, the communists were condemned to contentious interactions and continuing impotence.

On January 1, 1959, hundreds of communists were arrested and imprisoned and a campaign of sustained repression was implemented whose goal was the complete destruction of Egyptian Marxism. The communists were stunned, first by the arrests, and second by the brutal treatment they received in prison. According to Muhammad Sid Ahmad, no one in the movement expected Nasser to behave so harshly since the left had undertaken to endorse the government, and even when it was critical of individual policies of the regime, it was done within a line of general support.[56] Nasser, nevertheless, resented what he perceived to be the communists' disloyalty, and through imprisonment and torture he intended to put an end to organized Marxism in the country. His plans were not altered even after September 1961 when Syria withdrew from the union and Nasser was forced to reassess his policies.

During the summer of 1961 Nasser conducted a comprehensive

reevaluation of his strength and took a hard look at the direction in which the revolution was moving. A turning point had occurred in his regime. In July he announced massive nationalizations which he expected would reconstruct the economy in the national interest. In May 1962 he published the National Charter which explained his intention to bring about Arab socialism. From this document arose the Arab Socialist Union, the newly constituted official party of Egypt. As a result of his travels, discussions with Third World leaders, and broad readings, Nasser had come to admire the concept of "scientific socialism" by this time. Ironically, though, socialism was being carried out for him by people who were still predisposed to capitalism in a society in which communists were being actively persecuted.[57] And despite the development of his ideas and the advance of his reformist programs, Nasser never accommodated himself to the Marxist organizations which he always identified as potential challenges to his rule.

The communists, though in prison at this time, were acutely aware of the changes taking place in society. With information supplied by contraband radios and illegally acquired newspapers, discussions were abundant and evaluations of the regime were formulated.

The DMNL developed a theory relating to the situation. It declared that although a bourgeois state existed, there was a genuine socialist group at its head, led by Nasser, which was moving Egypt toward socialism. As such, it deserved Marxist endorsement. In contrast, the mainstream of the United Communist Party of Egypt evaluated the regime as state monopoly capitalist; since state control was all-consuming and the democratic dimension lacking, it recommended only conditional support. This position conflicted with the analysis of Fuad Mursi and Ismail Sabri Abd Allah, the traditional leaders of the ECP, who found themselves in a minority position on the issue. They considered Nasser to be the representative of the national bourgeoisie – an independent and anti-imperialist leader, but an antipopular ruler at the same time. They accepted alliances as appropriate under the circumstances, but strongly criticized Nasser's antipopular stances. Although these positions point to differences in the analysis of the class basis of the regime, they did not detract from the communists' general support of the government. Indeed, many communists still looked forward to productive cooperation with Nasserists which one day, it was hoped, might lead to an organic fusion between the regime and the left. But because these discussions were carried out in an environment of enforced alienation from the actual political situation, the communists were reduced to theorizing about reality, but not changing it.

In 1963 and 1964, the communists were completing their prison terms and being discharged from captivity. A catalyst for their timely release was Khrushchev's upcoming visit to Cairo to repair the tattered relations between Egypt and the Soviet Union. At that time, Nasser was seeking new alliances both domestically and internationally. He wanted relations with the Eastern Bloc improved. He wanted a realignment at home because since 1961 he had been losing the support of certain sectors of society, particularly the members of the bourgeoisie. He now needed to ally with advocates of social change to ensure the success and continuation of his policies. He hoped that the communists would provide him the backing he desired but he wanted to develop this on his own terms. With the idea of creating some form of cooperation with the left, Nasser established the secret party called the Vanguard Organization. This was to be the core structure of the Arab Socialist Union, Nasser's first real party, his loyal support, and his ideological arm. Some of the high communist intellectuals were to be brought into the Organization after they were freed from prison with the intention of absorbing and co-opting them, thereby disallowing any independent or oppositional activity.

When the communists were about to be released from the prisons and concentration camps, they held the illusion that they were entering a socialist society in which Marxists would assume an integral position. They expected to cooperate with Nasser and play an important role in forging the new society. The Marxists believed that the country was being remolded toward a new goal, and that soon a regime unambiguously identified with the masses would emerge.

When both the United Communist Party of Egypt and the DMNL decided independently to dissolve their organizations in 1965 and work with the regime, they believed they could best defend their ideas and contribute to defining the new society under the banner of Nasser's socialism. Of course, there were also practical pressures from the regime to dissolve. Nasser sent representatives who were friends of the leftists—Khalid Muhyi al-Din, Ahmad Hamrush, and Ibrahim Saad al-Din—to appeal to the communists to renounce secret activity.[58] The left was reminded that since most every Egyptian communist was known to the authorities, they would be unable to undertake oppositional political activity. But what proved decisive to the Marxists was the idea that socialism was possible in Egypt through Nasser's leadership. As a result, the communists did not think dissolution meant forsaking everything they had stood for. Rather, they believed they were beginning a new stage of political activity and moving toward a future which held promises of reform and development.[59]

Not long after accepting their freedom, however, it became apparent that there was a limit to Nasser's receptiveness to leftist ideas and restraints upon the policies he could adopt. Despite the nationalization measures, the promises of the National Charter, and the acceptance of so-called scientific socialism, Nasser accomplished only limited socialist measures and never forsook his distrust of pluralism. He rejected any dealings with an organized communist movement and agreed to work only with selected individual Marxists.

The communists felt betrayed. The "socialist society" they were admitted to was only a shell of what they had expected, and most found themselves with no jobs, no money, no homes, no political activity, and no place to turn. Moreover, many felt wronged by the small number of highly intellectual comrades who were awarded important positions in society, mainly through the Vanguard Organization. The more upper-class cadres, who had university training and the kinds of skills Nasser needed to support his new programs, were channeled into important jobs in the media, in business, and in government. In contrast, members of the rank and file, and particularly the workers, harbored the view that their dreams, their movement, and their futures had been sacrificed for the benefit of the leftist elite.

While in prison, isolated from the core of activity, the communists could not develop a realistic assessment of the regime. Separated from society, they became overly optimistic about Egypt's future development, the changes being instituted, and the radicalization of the leadership. They were unable to recognize how strong the forces of opposition to socialism were and did not understand the bourgeois class character of the Nasserist movement in which strong tendencies toward conservatism prevailed.

The limited cooperation between Nasser and the communists did produce the monthly magazine *al-Talia*, which was designed as a forum for Marxist ideas. The members of the editorial board were mainly Marxists, and the editor-in-chief, Lutfi al-Kholi, continually worked to keep the magazine independent from the regime. The intention of the board was to provide analyses of Egyptian society which would contribute to a deeper understanding of the country and encourage economic, social, and political reform.

Although the Marxists had imagined that the dissolution of their parties would remove old constraints and create new political opportunities, their hopes were not fulfilled. In reality, Nasser contained the communists, kept a watchful eye over them, and very cunningly co-opted them. Nasser needed the communists after 1961, but because he was always deeply suspicious of their loyalty to him, he exploited their abilities and talents as individuals, while making absolutely certain that the movement itself was dismantled. He destroyed communism organizationally and prevented the Marxists from functioning as a viable political alternative.

6

The Significance of the Egyptian Communist Movement

Nasser used to say of Marxism something very interesting in his last years. He used to say that it is a factor to enrich us and to correct our mistakes. . . . It is a factor that allows us to avoid pitfalls and gives us a view richer than a purely nationalist one. In other words, we deal with Marxists as consultants, for enriching and consulting . . . as "signals" of possible things that could evolve.[1]

GAMAL ABDUL NASSER could think of the Marxists as useful consultants rather than as threatening rivals because, in fact, they never were a serious threat to him: they never created a mass movement, never diffused their ideas widely, and were never prepared to take power. Because the communist movement of the 1940s and early 1950s was divided into a multiplicity of political parties, the message it issued was disjointed. Inflexibility, misguided beliefs in ideological purity, political differences, and personal hostility, not only prevented the Marxists from creating a single communist party which could unite all the diverse trends, but it also involved the left in internecine squabbles which undermined its effectiveness. Sectarianism splintered the Egyptian communist movement. The disputes which arose between the competing organizations were only inadequately resolved and, left to smolder, they were often reignited sometime in the future causing further damage to the movement. As a result of distrust and competition, the early separations that characterized the movement in the 1940s continued on and prevented a lasting merger of the groups from ever taking place. Often deeply embroiled in interparty conflicts, Egyptian communists sometimes lost sight of the

149

larger goal—the fundamental transformation of society. The revolution they discussed, debated, wrote about, and fought for remained
a revolution in theory only.

Although one of the basic questions the Egyptian communists
theoretically grappled with was how to get people to take matters
into their own hands, how to develop local leaderships capable of
understanding area problems and working with supporters toward the
realization of local improvements, the communists never developed
a political program that could capture the mass of Egyptians. With
some exceptions, they were unable to effectively move out of the political center of Cairo and outside the social strata of urban students,
professionals, and skilled workers. This narrowness fatally limited the
movement. Despite well intentioned efforts, with few notable exceptions, communists could not penetrate the rural villages or the poor
urban neighborhoods. The predominantly petty-bourgeois communists always remained deeply estranged from the lived reality of the
humble Egyptians who, in theory, were to be the backbone of their
movement. The Marxists were never able to transform their message
of popular participation in the political process into concrete activity. They were an extraparliamentary opposition which functioned
on the periphery of Egyptian politics and society.

The ideas championed by intellectual Egyptian communists were
not in themselves antipathetic to the masses. But because communist ideology failed to offer the masses a program of action to which
they could commit themselves, their theory seemed little more than
mere abstraction to the majority of the population. Thus, Marxism
never became a mobilizing force in Egypt.

The Marxists had also to contend with the Wafd which, since
its inception, played a recognized and highly significant role in the
nationalist struggle for independence. While the communists viewed
independence as an issue of paramount importance, they could never
assume for themselves the role of the nationalist vanguard. The Wafd
was a prominent parliamentary force and even though it became increasingly moderate with regard to the King and the British in the
1940s, it retained its credibility among the population as the major
proponent of Egyptian self-rule. Moreover, because the Wafd was able
to attract support from a variety of followers, the communist movement suffered. For instance, the left's commitment to a united front
strategy was never attainable because a large number of typically bourgeois and petty-bourgeois nationalists found expression for their
political aspirations in the Wafd. As a result, the battle for national

independence in Egypt in the 1940s took a parliamentary, not a revolutionary course.

Had the communist movement been allowed to function legally and within the framework of mainstream politics, perhaps competition among parties, experience with elections, and a knowledge of mass organization on the scale of the Wafd, would have animated political life in Egypt and given the left an opportunity to grow. Since Marxism was forced to operate underground it was given neither the chance to make its message nationally known nor to develop a measure of credibility which could have won it adherents.

The communist model was understandably not attractive to most Egyptians. To aristocrats, large landowners, men of religion, and capitalists it symbolized disaster. To peasants, the administrative petty bourgeoisie, small merchants, and unorganized workers, it was simply unintelligible. The upper classes may have feared communism, but the majority of the population was too uninformed to comprehend it or too close to the margin of subsistence to even think about it. That the model was compelling to intellectuals reflected their access to modern and imported ideas and their desire to change the kind of society in which they lived.

According to revolutionary intellectuals, independence, industrialization, parliamentarianism, and equality could be achieved only by overthrowing the established ruling class and replacing it with a radical leadership which could build a broadly based class alliance. But the Egyptian communists never produced a plan to accomplish this. Essentially, this reduced Marxism to a fringe opposition force whose propaganda efforts—which were directed to the upper levels of the society—proved to be its most lasting contribution. The communists may have talked at great length about toppling the establishment and assuming power, but they never actively sought to replace the regime with a Marxist organization. Instead, they concentrated on more limited victories by influencing groups of intellectuals and professionals, students in schools and universities, workers in factories, and soldiers in the military.

Arguably, the left forfeited the two most promising opportunities for taking power—in 1946 when the dynamic nationalist movement turned away from the mainstream of the Wafd in search of a new leadership, and in 1951 when guerrilla warfare against the British activated the population in a campaign to oust the occupier from the Nile Valley. Although Marxists participated in the activity of the time and even generated militant behavior, they failed to harness national frustrations. This reflected both the left's incomplete strategy for taking hold of the reins of the government and its own ideological purity. It was not enough that the communists criticized the status quo, agitated against it, and advocated reforms. The absence of concrete plans for replacing the existing government with a communist one suggests the remoteness of the left's chances for seizing real power.

Despite all this, Egyptian communism has had a surprisingly enduring presence in the political arena. It has faced and withstood factionalism, police repression, ideological confusion, and numerical insignificance. In the 1940s and 1950s, it constituted an oppositional force worthy of note because it exerted a traceable influence on Egyptian intellectual and political life, primarily through its contribution to journalism, poetry, short-story writing, philosophical and political publications, and through its participation in demonstrations and strikes. Unfailingly, the communists were present at key moments of nationalist, student, and trade union militancy. Sometimes in the vanguard of radical activity and other times in the background, the activists were always found in steady support of social reform movements. Whether in the streets protesting political corruption or the absence of governmental accountability, or in the schools and universities debating their vision of a new future, or in the trade unions demanding basic reforms, the communists gave voice to the dissatisfactions and disappointments of the population at large.

The Marxists operated according to three basic but significant ideas: the inability of the Wafd to achieve national independence; the importance of a politically independent popular movement; and the necessity of internationalizing the Egyptian cause. These guiding principles gave them a place in the nationalist movement during its revival in the mid-1940s and kept them active into the 1950s.

Early in the movement, the communists criticized the Wafdist leadership for that party's failure to realize the goal of national independence. During World War II, and in the postwar period, the Wafd was mellowing and, as a reflection of its more affluent and conservative membership, becoming less confrontational. Communist handbills and newspaper articles emphasized the vacillations of the Wafd and its seeming powerlessness to extract compromises from the British, thereby partially undermining the hegemony of the Wafd and its ideology of negotiation, especially in the latter 1940s.

The communists repeatedly stressed the primacy of the popular movement and the centrality of the class struggle. Through their literature they defended national and democratic rights and discredited traditional political parties and their claims to represent the interests of the entire population. Again, the ideological assault was partly successful: the Wafdist claim to represent all Egyptians, indivisibly, was no longer uncritically accepted.

Endeavoring to internationalize the Egyptian cause, the communists brought Egypt's demand for national independence and political freedom to the attention of the world community. By attending international conferences and supporting radical international bodies, the communists intended to show the world that Egypt was entitled to its national liberation. While this behavior might have embarrassed the British, it did not, ultimately, bring Egypt closer to self-government.

Marxist articulation of these ideas contributed to the destabilization of the constitutional monarchy and diluted the strength of the increasingly worn-out Wafd party, once the dominant nationalist force in the country. It helped make conditions ripe for the repudiation of liberalism and the inauguration of the Nasser era. While the communists did not alter the structure of Egyptian society themselves, their intense campaigning among students, intellectuals, and groups of workers did advance the collapse of the traditional political structure. The political work carried out by the left and the ideological positions it propagated helped create a climate favorable to the emergence of Gamal Abdul Nasser and the Free Officers Movement in 1952. Partly as a result of communist propaganda, liberal nationalism was no longer the only language of Egyptian political discourse. As a consequence of the destabilization of liberal ideology, when the Free Officers accomplished their coup d'etat they received widespread popular support. While the communists looked forward to still more momentous changes in Egyptian life—which they themselves hoped to inspire—perhaps the greatest irony of the movement was that its successes were not found in their socialist revolution but were realized incrementally in the policies carried out after the left was decimated following Nasser's coup d'etat. The removal of the British, skepticism of the West, land reform, nationalization, alliance with the Socialist bloc countries, and socialist economic planning were all communist supported and articulated ideas which Nasser cleverly adopted to his own, non-Marxist goals. Nasser's accomplishments domestically in eliminating the vestiges of feudalism, improving education, housing, and working conditions, negotiating a British withdrawal, and his initiatives in the international arena as a leader of the non-aligned movement, reduced the appeal of the communist model. Nasser's selective use of communist talent, moreover, divided the left between those who focused on the progressive elements of Nasserism and those who viewed authoritarianism and repression as the signal characteristics of Nasser's regime.

After the coup d'etat, the DMNL and the Workers' Vanguard were prepared to compromise with the military regime in the hope that the new policy-makers would favor radical improvements in Egyptian society and broader based international alliances. They applauded the passing of new legislation which bettered working conditions and increased the minimum wage, but recognized that while the regime's intention was to accomplish reform it would ultimately do so by eliminating communist influence in trade unions, student organizations, and professional groups. Their relatively positive disposition toward the new regime—which contrasted to that of the ECP—was not reciprocated. After Nasser assumed full control of the regime, he imprisoned members of the left, particularly those with ties to the labor movement. Communist backing wavered in consequence.

After the 1955 Bandung Conference, the Czech arms deal, and the tripartite attack against Egypt, a reassessment by all communists in Egypt produced a platform of general support for the regime. Nasser recognized this position and allowed the communists to function relatively openly until the clash over the Egyptian-Syrian union. Ultimately, communist support for the new government in Iraq ended the tentative rapprochement. A wave of arrests followed which put virtually the entire Egyptian communist movement behind bars for up to five years. As a result, between 1959 and 1964, the communist presence in Egypt was restricted to the prisons and concentration camps scattered through the country.

Nonetheless, even inside the prison walls, the communists were active. They provided their cadres with education and training, held continuous discussions, and initiated debates with oppositional groups. Despite the hardships of incarceration, the communists continued to support the government's antiimperialist stands, endorsed the nationalization orders which went into effect in 1961, and became convinced that Egypt was moving slowly down the road to socialist development.

From early in his regime, Nasser was interested in the ideas of the communists. Even when they were imprisoned, Nasser deemed the leftists ideologically significant. According to Muhammad Sid Ahmad:

When we communists were in prison in the Wahat, the Oasis, very often the police used to come into our cells. They probably had agents inside the prison. We used to hide our documents in our cells by removing certain stones. When the police would come, they would go right to the hiding place and take our documents away to the President of the Republic. We were in prison; we had no physical contacts with the realities outside. It was assumed we had no pencil, paper, or newspapers. We were not to know anything. But we got to know things because we smuggled in transistor radios and we used to listen to everything. . . . There were no trials over the documents which the police seized. They were not interested in this aspect. They were only interested in probing our minds. We were the "signals" even there.[2]

In 1964, Khrushchev scheduled a visit to Cairo in an effort to improve Soviet-Egyptian relations. This was about the time when the communists' prison sentences were nearing an end. Uneasy about the number of imprisoned leftists in the country, Nasser arranged to have them released in return for certain conditions being met. The communists were told to dissolve their organizations and become integrated into the mainstream of Egyptian intellectual, political, and social life. Because of self-preservation and an expectation that cooperation between the forces of communism and Nasserism was possible, the communists "voluntarily" dissolved their organizations. In recompense, Nasser brought dozens of Marxists into the bureaucracy, the media, the Arab Socialist Union, and the Ministries of Education and Planning.

Individual, well-placed Marxists imagined that they would assist in the restructuring of society. They took the announcement of the magazine *al-Talia*, for example, as an indication that the regime wanted to know about and understand communist inspired ideas. *Al-Talia* did become an important theoretical journal in Egypt, and within its pages Marxist studies predominated. The editorial board felt confident enough, in fact, to forward a so-called "independent platform," in an effort to distance the magazine from the regime and offer a more radical plan for Egyptian development. But this was the extent of its radical activity. Ultimately, Nasser paralyzed the Marxists by repressing and co-opting them, and by exploiting the abilities and ideas of a few individuals. Through this strategy he broke the communists, and for the decade between 1965 and 1975 there was no independent Marxist political activity in Egypt.

When Anwar Sadat came to power, the communists were divided in their attitude toward the new regime, but the general consensus was that Sadat would continue the policies of the previous government. In fact, some prominent communists such as Fuad Mursi and Ismail Sabri Abd Allah joined Sadat's government, and only made a full break with Sadat in 1975 after the policy of economic liberalism, to attract foreign investment, was instituted. But for most leftists the break with Sadat came earlier, certainly after the 1973 war with Israel brought him in close cooperation with the United States. By this time, Sadat's vision of Egypt had become the antithesis of Nasser's, and his policies represented a clean break with the Nasserist tradition. As a result, conditions were ripe for the revival of the Egyptian Communist Party. This occurred in 1975 when the earlier decision to disband the party was declared no longer correct. The party was revived as an active, though underground organization.

The communist movement continues to exist in Egypt today, but its effect is minimal largely because it has perpetuated the tradition established in the 1940s: it is fragmented into different and competing groups which are widely separated from the mass of Egyptian society. It has not found a language in which to speak to the population of Egypt, nor the policies to attract more than a small number of committed activists. Moreover, the legal leftist opposition party, al-Tagammu, has absorbed many radical Egyptians who have come to believe that significant change can be accomplished only by assembling democrats, Marxists, Nasserists, and independents into a united force against the present regime.

Appendix
Journalistic Literature

To survey the political aspirations of the communists without examining the forms of their ideological expression is to study only part of the subject. A review of the journalistic literature written and read by the left from World War II until the 1952 coup d'etat will reveal the influences that helped shape oppositional culture.

During and after World War II the pattern of intellectual life was changing in Egypt. The inherent tensions of the society were accentuated by war and there was increased local attention both to the everyday problems affecting the population and the seemingly intractable British occupation. During the 1940s the new wave of books which embraced a radical social and economic bent, the newspapers which espoused oppositional ideas, and the new poetry and literature which were published contributed to radical thoughts about Egypt's future. This was a decade of relative openness when a wide range of ideas were expressed and the reading public was exposed to differences in political and cultural opinions.

Newspapers represented part of the avant-garde radicalism of the 1940s. The left press, on the whole, was well written and geared to a general readership. The attention the oppositional press paid to both style and content was perhaps the result of having to compete with the developed and sophisticated style of journalism found in *al-Ahram, al-Wafd al-Misri, Roz al-Yusuf* and other established publications.

The legal left press provided a forum for dissident or controversial ideas. It served as a method of outreach, spreading the nationalist message of struggle against foreign imperialism. Not only was it a legal platform for clandestine organizations, but it was also an important means of diffusing Marxist consciousness and attracting adherents into the radical underground. Indeed, because of the prominence of the leftist publications and the outstanding journalists who wrote for them, the impression was created that the communist movement was larger than it really was.[1]

These "lesser" periodicals of the time, many of which will be discussed

157

below, provide important insights into local activity, intellectual trends, and the Egyptian analysis of the international situation. This is an important medium for understanding how the dissident movement conceived of the problems of Egyptian society and how it proposed to solve them.[2]

Al-Tatawwur

The first number of *al-Tatawwur* (Evolution) was published in January 1940 by Georges Henein who financed the periodical, Anwar Kamil, who was editor-in-chief, and Ramsis Yunan, Kamil al-Tilmisani, and Albert Cossery who were contributing editors. A sophisticated journal which represented a new trend in Egypt's literary, political, and artistic life, *al-Tatawwur* printed a wide range of articles reflecting the diverse ideological visions of its contributors. The message of the magazine was the reformation of Egypt's moral, social, and economic systems so that the majority of people would not continue to live in poverty, ignorance, and sickness.

The magazine did not tout a doctrinaire party line, though it was the organ of the Trotskyite group Bread and Freedom. No program was offered to solve problems or raise the cultural level of the population. Instead, the magazine was conceived as a forum for rising intellectuals to express their reformist cultural and political ideas. *Al-Tatawwur* provided an opportunity for a new generation of leftist writers to address problems in Egyptian society.

Al-Majalla al-Jadida

Al-Majalla al-Jadida (The New Review) was a magazine first published by Salama Musa during the late 1920s and 1930s focusing on politics, social reform, education, and psychology. It dominated the liberal cultural scene from about 1928 to 1935, after which the ideas of Salama Musa played a less conspicuous role in Egyptian political life.[3]

By December 7, 1942, there were discernible changes in the magazine: it was longer in form; its contributors had changed and at various times included Ramsis Yunan, Mustafa Kamil Munib, and Kamil al-Tilmisani; and its articles were more politically controversial. From about 1942/43, the magazine concentrated on articles dealing with politics, art, literature, and poetry, all of which were seen as vehicles of social protest. A new breed of socialist publicists took over the journal and revised it to reflect their own views.

The reason why Salama Musa transferred the magazine to Ramsis Yunan and his colleagues is yet to be established. Anwar Kamil, who knew Salama Musa and was connected with Yunan and Henein, speculated that Salama Musa may have had financial problems preventing him from continuing the journal independently.[4] Louis Awad agreed with this analysis. According to Awad, Salama Musa inherited forty *faddans* of land from his father. In order to support the magazine he was forced to sell one *faddan* after another, and, ultimately, "he lost his fortune for culture." Though he was not bankrupt, he sacrificed his resources to meet the expenses of the journal.[5]

In 1943, the magazine published articles on philosophy, culture, art, science, and social reform. The war was also a major concern and interest was shown in the Soviet Union's efforts against fascism. *Al-Majalla al-Jadida* was not an organ of any one political party but rather a platform from which young intellectuals spoke. It called for progress in the solution of Egypt's political and social problems, the struggle against fascism, the end to imperialism and the economic inferiority it presupposed, the establishment of democracy, and the creation of an educated society.

Al-Talia

The magazine *al-Talia* (The Vanguard) was first published on September 15, 1945, by the Union of University Graduates, a radical youth group. Articles were generally written by professors and students and concentrated on Arab unity, Palestine, the economic effects of occupation, and women. From its fourth issue, the names of communist writers began to appear. By its sixth, on March 15, 1946, the radical inclination of the journal was evident when Abd al-Rahman al-Sharqawi, later an accomplished novelist, assumed the post of editor-in-chief.

The magazine was important because it represented a forward-looking trend in the thoughts of university students. Although it did not exhibit a coherent political line, its merit lay in its ability to diffuse radical ideas and demonstrate to the public the antinationalist character of the government.[6]

Al-Ahd al-Jadid

The newspaper *al-Ahd al-Jadid* (The New Era) had a varied history. When it was first published in 1936 by Mahmud Abd al-Malik Quraytim, who was a member of the Liberal Constitutionalist Party, it specialized in auction advertisements and lost article notices.[7] By the end of 1943, however, the paper had begun to report on workers' issues from a conciliatory perspective. According to the paper, workers had rights, but they had to take advantage of them patiently and moderately, and not engage in strikes or work stoppages.

On December 18, 1943, *al-Ahd al-Jadid* described itself as a "newspaper of freedom and the organ of workers and all popular classes." From January 8, 1944, the publication dealt almost exclusively with workers' concerns: the cost of living, labor legislation, trade union news, and the cooperative movement. It became a syndicalist-centered movement.

The paper's orientation changed once again on December 17, 1944, when an editorial, for the first time, discussed the relationship between workers and politics, modifying the previous suggestion that politics and unionism did not mix. In 1945, the tabloid assumed an even more political stance when it printed articles about Stalin and the Soviet Union. By August 1945 the paper announced, "we express the opinion of the workers on different problems; we fight tyranny and oppression which bloc the working class in its daily life." It called for independence and democracy as the representative of workers and nationalists. Inexplicably, in October 1945 the newspaper reverted to a Liberal Constitutionalist, pro-Sidqi line.

Al-Fajr al-Jadid

Al-Fajr al-Jadid (The New Dawn) was first published in May 1945 by communist intellectuals Ahmad Sadiq Saad, Yusuf Darwish, Raymond Duwayk, and Ahmad Rushdi Salih. First a fortnightly magazine, by the end of 1945 it became, with some lapses, a weekly publication. It reported on issues vital to Egypt's development: foreign control over the Egyptian economy; the freeing of the Egyptian pound from the English pound sterling; imperialism; democracy; and education. The magazine defended Arab unity and contributed to laying the foundations of a new school in art and poetry. Critiques of the cinema industry in Egypt, modern Egyptian literature, and the newest poems of Abd al-Rahman al-Sharqawi, Kamal Abd al-Halim, Muhammad Khalil Qasim, and Mahmud Tawfiq were printed. It was a nationalist publication whose scope included literary and political journalism.

Al-Damir

Yusuf Darwish, a trade union lawyer, along with Mahmud al-Askari, Yusuf al-Mudarrik, and Taha Saad Uthman, three prominent labor leaders, published the workers' newspaper *al-Damir* (The Conscience). The organ of the Workers' Committee of National Liberation, *al-Damir* urged workers to establish independent labor and political platforms. It stressed trade union rights and responsibilities, the necessity of organizing international labor solidarity, and the importance of establishing ties among Arab workers.

Hurriyat al-Shuub

Hurriyat al-Shuub (The Freedom of the People) was published during the 1930s as a nonpolitical literary and cultural magazine. Then, on February 11, 1942, a significant change in the journal occurred and articles of a social and political orientation were published, including columns on: education, parliamentarianism, the life of the agricultural worker, democracy, women's rights, workers' and trade union affairs, and the Sudan. The names of socialist journalists began to appear and included Abdu Dhahab Hasanayn, Mustafa Kamil Munib, Salih Arabi, Sayyid Khayyal, and Kamil al-Tilmisani. *Hurriyat al-Shuub* was a reformist magazine, but it had connections with Henri Curiel, as indicated by advertisements featuring his left-wing bookstore, al-Midan.

Like other publications of this period, however, the political line was not consistent over time: it was moderate, moved in a radical direction, then reverted. In 1943 the magazine again changed its policy and revealed first a Wafdist inclination and then its support for the Palace. By 1944 the articles were no longer oppositional at all. Publication stopped on April 1, 1945, and then *al-Mustaqbal* (The Future) was published in its stead between April 20, 1945, and August 21, 1946. This change was merely nominal.

Umdurman

Umdurman, which was published between March 15, 1945, and July 1, 1946, was essentially a Sudanese newspaper for the Sudanese living in Egypt. The emphasis of the paper was on Sudanese society, its economic and political future after the war, and Sudanese folk traditions. But, in addition, the experiences of Sudanese students in Egypt were also documented. The magazine, under the control of Henri Curiel, was owned by Muhammad Amin Husayn al-Muhami and was edited by Abdu Dhahab Hasanayn and included a support staff of members of the EMNL. It contained an editorial column, pages of news and political commentary, a women's section, a students' section, poems, scientific articles, and art and music reviews. The journal advocated the common struggle of Egypt and Sudan against the British and the right of the Sudanese to national self-determination.

Al-Jamahir

Al-Jamahir (The Masses) was a vibrant political newspaper which operated from April 1947 until its license was confiscated by the government on May 15, 1948, when martial law was announced in Egypt. The paper originated as the organ of Iskra but after the establishment of the DMNL it became the latter's voice. *Al-Jamahir* was a socialist publication which emphasized the battle for economic, cultural, and political liberation from imperialism, and called for democracy, civil rights, and a decent standard of living for all.

Both local and international articles appeared and covered such topics as Egyptian rural poverty, the failure of the mainstream political parties to achieve independence and national development, and comparative reports about the United States, France, Yugoslavia, Palestine, and Czechoslovakia. Articles dedicated to the concerns of women were published and the journal opened its pages to young leftist poets.

Al-Bashir

Al-Bashir (The Messenger) was a left-Wafdist political newspaper with some connection to the DMNL through its editor Fathi al-Ramli. Between April 11, 1950, and December 4, 1950, the paper had a leftist bent and appealed mainly to a leftist audience. Many of the issues which the paper addressed were of concern to both communists and left-Wafdists and included: poverty in Egypt; the nationalization of transport, water, and sugar as a means of national development; women's rights; progressive taxation; trade union affairs; peace; and the struggle against imperialism. There were articles dealing with the Korean War and China, and there were poems by Kamal Abd al-Halim, (under the pseudonym of Muhammad Kamal). When the newspaper became particularly critical of the Wafdist government, its publication was halted by the government.

Al-Malayin

Al-Malayin (The Millions) was an organ of the DMNL in 1951. Its owner and editor-in-chief was Ahmad Sadiq Azzam. Some of its principal writers were Ibrahim Abd al-Halim, Enayet al-Halim, Rashid al-Barawi, Abd al-Murni al-Said, and Yusuf Hilmi. A typical issue contained reports about peasants, women, workers, international liberation struggles, art, theater, literature, and sports.

Al-Katib

Al-Katib (The Scribe) the organ of the Egyptian Peace Supporters, was first published on May 5, 1951. Primarily concerned with issues of international peace, it also published Muhammad Yusuf al-Mudarrik's articles on workers; columns on democratic freedoms and the defense of political prisoners; and poems by Zaki Murad and Kamal Abd al-Halim. Lutfi al-Kholi, a friend of the Marxist left, wrote a regular piece, and Bindari Pasha, the former Egyptian ambassador to the Soviet Union, published his memoirs in it. Many photographs were published which documented the gruesome effects of war.

Al-Wajib

On September 10, 1952, the liberal newspaper *al-Wajib* (The Duty) began publishing articles on working class issues. By October 22, 1952, the paper was calling for national liberation, peace, popular democracy, nuclear disarmament, and a return to parliamentary life. Some of its contributors included Ahmad Sadiq Azzam, Ibrahim Abd al-Halim, Muhammad al-Bindari, Sid Turk, Yusuf Hilmi, and Ahmad Taha. The newspaper was closed down by the military government on December 25, 1952.

Notes

Introduction

1. Asim al-Disuqi, *Kibar mullak al-aradi al-ziraiyya wa dawruhum fi al-mujtama al-misri, 1914–1952* (Cairo, 1975), 20.

1—The Roots of Egyptian Communism

1. Hanna Batatu, *The Old Social Classes and the Revolutionary Movements of Iraq* (Princeton, Princeton University Press, 1978), 374–75.

2. Rifaat al-Said, *Tarikh al-haraka al-ishtirakiyya fi misr, 1900–1925* (Cairo, 1975), 161.

3. Mona Hammam, "Women Workers and the Practice of Freedom as Education: The Egyptian Experience" (Ph.D. Thesis, University of Kansas, 1977), 118.

4. Batatu, *Social Classes*, 387–88.

5. M. S. Agwani, *Communism in the Arab East* (New York, Asia Publishing House, 1969), 4–5.

6. My comments on the rebirth of Egyptian Marxism during the 1930s are based, in part, on Rifaat al-Said's works, *al-Yasar al-misri, 1925–1940* (Beirut, 1972) and *Tarikh al-munazzamat al-yasariyya al-misriyya, 1940–1950* (Cairo, 1976).

7. Rifaat al-Said's interviews with Raymond Aghion, April 4, 1975, Paris, and Ahmad Sadiq Saad, April 6, 1975, Cairo, transcripts of the meetings provided to the author.

8. Rifaat al-Said's interview with Raymond Aghion, April 4, 1975, Paris, transcript of the meeting provided to the author.

9. Rifaat al-Said's interview with Dina Forti, February 24, 1975, Paris, transcript of the meeting provided to the author.

10. Ahmad Sadiq Saad, *Safahat min al-yasar al-misri* (Cairo, 1976), 43–45.

11. Hilary Wayment, ed., *Egypt Now* (Cairo, Le Groupe Études, 1942).

12. Ibid., 54.

13. al-Said, *Tarikh al-Munazzamat*, 170.

14. Personal interview with Hilmi Yassin, December 23, 1979, Cairo.

165

15. Saad, *Safahat*, 45.

16. Judicial inquiry of Anwar Kamil before the High Military Prosecutor in the Case of Socialism and the Bread and Freedom group, Cairo, 1942, (in Arabic).

17. *al-Tatawwur*, March, 1940.

18. Ibid., February 1940.

19. Ibid., May 1940.

20. Ibid., January 1940.

21. The well-known trade union leader Muhammad Ali Amr joined the group in its earliest days.

22. Judicial Inquiry of Anwar Kamil, 1942.

23. Louis Awad, "Dikrayat Baida," in *Hommage à Georges Henein* (Le Caire, Le Part du Sable, 1974), 122.

2—A Portrait of the Communist Movement

1. For more information about the student movement in Egypt, see Ahmed Abdalla, *The Student Movement and National Politics in Egypt* (London, Al Saqi Books, 1985).

2. Jean-Pierre Thieck, "La journée du 21 Févriér 1946 dans l'histoire du mouvement national Égyptien," Diplôme d'études superieures en histoire, Université de Paris VIII, 1974, 165.

3. Abd al-Munim al-Ghazzali, *Tarikh al-haraka al-niqabiyya al-misriyya, 1889–1952* (Cairo, 1968) 205–7.

4. Personal interview with Fuad Mursi, November 12, 1979, Cairo.

5. Raoul Makarious, *La Jeunesse Intellectualle d'Égypte au Lendemain de la Deuxième Guerre Mondiale* (Paris, Mouton, 1960), 45, 50–52.

6. Afaf Lutfi al-Sayyid Marsot, "The Revolutionary Gentlewomen in Egypt," in Lois Beck and Nikki Keddie, eds., *Women in the Muslim World* (Cambridge, Mass., Harvard University Press, 1978), 261–76.

7. Personal interview with Inge Aflatun, January 5, 1980, Cairo.

8. Personal interview with Latifa al-Zayat, February 9, 1980, Cairo.

9. Civil Court, Case no. 1949, Abdin, year 1947, 55 (in Arabic).

10. Personal interview with Soraya Adham, May 20, 1980, Cairo.

11. *Ahdafna*, original pamphlet from the League of Women Students and Graduates from the University and Egyptian Institutes, Cairo, 1946.

12. Personal interview with Latifa al-Zayat, February 9, 1980, Cairo.

13. *Ahdafna*.

14. Personal interview with Latifa al-Zayat, February 9, 1980, Cairo.

15. Gudrun Krämer's work on the Egyptian Jewish community, soon to be translated from German into English, may be consulted for further information in connection with Jews who became communists.

16. RG 319 431882, December 22, 1947. U.S. National Archives and Records Service.

17. Personal interview with Shahata Harun, January 9, 1980, Cairo.

18. The *galabiyya* is the free-flowing gown worn by Egyptian men especially from the lower classes.

19. Personal interview with Raymond Stambouli, June 4, 1980, Paris.

20. Ibid.

21. Marcel Israel, "Esquisse Historique de Mouvement Communiste Égyptien," Report presented to the Italian Communist Party, n.d., 18, (photocopy).

22. Personal interview with Shahata Harun, January 9, 1980, Cairo.

23. Personal interview with Aime Beresi, September 24, 1979, Paris.

24. Personal interview with Albert Arie, May 13, 1980, Cairo.

25. Henri Curiel, *Pages Auto-Biographiques*, (Digne, Association Henri Curiel, 1977), 116.

3—The Historical Development of the Egyptian Communist Movement, 1942–1947

1. Quoted in Jean and Simmone Lacouture, *Egypt in Transition* (New York, Criterion Books, 1958), 257.

2. Thieck, "La journée," 21.

3. Saad, *Safahat*, 31.

4. P. J. Vatikiotis, *The Modern History of Egypt* (London, Weidenfeld and Nicolson, 1969), 357.

5. al-Said, *Tarikh al-munazzamat*, 95.

6. Personal interview with Louis Awad, April 22, 1980, Cairo.

7. Lacouture, *Egypt*, 259.

8. Personal interview with Muhammad Yusuf al-Jindi, January 27, 1980, Cairo.

9. Civil Court, Case no. 1949, Abdin, year 1947, 956.

10. Quoted from Samuel Bardell, *A Note on the Funeral of Henri Curiel*, May, 1978.

11. Personal interview with Raymond Stambouli, June 4, 1980, Paris; Curiel, *Pages Auto-Biographiques*, 22–23.

12. Rifaat al-Said's interview with Henri Curiel, January 25, 1970, Paris, reprinted in Rifaat al-Said, *al-Yassar al-misri, 1925–1940* (Beirut, 1972), 284.

13. RG 319 232870, January 10, 1946. U.S. National Archives and Records Service.

14. Personal interview with Raymond Stambouli, June 4, 1980, Paris.

15. Personal interview with Rifaat al-Said, December 22, 1979, Cairo.

16. Personal interview with Raymond Stambouli, June 4, 1980, Paris.

17. Abdu Dhahab was also called Abd al-Latif Dhahab Hasanayn.

18. FO 371/46003 J2962/440/16, September 1, 1945. Great Britain, Public Records Office.

19. RG 319 232870, July 10, 1946. U.S. National Archives and Records Service.

20. Civil Court, Case no. 1949, Abdin, year 1947, 72–74.

21. Rauf Abbas, *al-Haraka al-ummaliyya fi misr, 1899–1952* (Cairo, 1967), 289.

22. Personal interview with Rifaat al-Said, December 22, 1979, Cairo.

23. Rifaat al-Said's interview with Mubarrak Abdu Fadl, December 29, 1974, Cairo, transcript of the meeting provided to the author.

24. Personal interview with Rifaat al-Said, December 22, 1979, Cairo.

25. Rifaat al-Said's interview with Mubarrak Abdu Fadl, December 29, 1974, Cairo, transcript of the meeting provided to the author.

26. Personal interview with Ahmad Hamrush, April 11, 1980, Cairo.

27. Civil Court, Case no. 1949, Abdin, year 1947, 72–73.

28. Personal interview with Muhammad Sid Ahmad, December 31, 1979, Cairo.

29. Rifaat al-Said's interview with Henri Curiel, February 4, 1973, Paris, transcript of the meeting provided to the author.

30. Civil Court, Case no. 1949, Abdin, year 1947, 46–48.

31. Ibid.

32. Personal interview with Muhammad Sid Ahmad, February 16, 1980, Cairo.

33. Ibid., December 13, 1979, Cairo.

34. Personal interview with Sharif Hatata, February 28, 1980, Cairo.

35. Personal interview with Latifa al-Zayat, February 9, 1980, Cairo.

36. Personal interview with Muhammad Sid Ahmad, December 13, 1979, Cairo.

37. Personal interview with Albert Arie, March 29, 1980, Cairo.

38. Personal interview with Sharif Hatata, February 28, 1980, Cairo.

39. Saad, *Safahat*, 48–49.

40. Thieck, "La journée," 77–78.

41. Tariq al-Bishri, *al-Haraka al-siyasiyya fi misr, 1945–1952* (Cairo, 1972), 156–57.

42. Ibid., 221.

43. *al-Fajr al-Jadid*, October 15, 1945.

44. Ibid, February 13, 1945.

45. Abbas, *al-Haraka al-ummaliyya fi misr*, 279.

46. Rifaat al-Said's interview with Ahmad Sadiq Saad, April 6, 1975, Cairo, transcript of the meeting provided to the author.

47. Personal interview with Hilmi Yassin, December 23, 1979, Cairo.

48. Ibid.

49. Civil Court, Case no. 2021, Misr Qadima, 247, year 1951, 131, (in Arabic).

50. Ibid., 177–87.

51. Ibid., 165–68.

52. Personal interview with Jamal Ghali, March 26, 1980, Cairo.

53. Thieck, "La journée," 175; Shuhdi Atiya al-Shafii, *Tatawwur al-haraka al-wataniyya al-misriyya, 1882–1956* (Cairo, 1956), 97–99.

54. Agwani, *Communism*, 44.

55. Rashed al-Barawi, *The Military Coup in Egypt* (Cairo, Renaissance Publishers, 1952), 150.

56. A. W. Sanson, *I Spied Spies* (London, Harrop, 1965), 197.

57. FO 141/1158 DS(E) 200/128 66/72/47, August 9, 1947. Great Britain, Public Records Office.

58. Personal interview with Soraya Adham, May 10, 1980, Cairo.

59. Anouar Abdel-Malek, *Egypt: Military Society, the Army Regime, the Left, and Social Change under Nasser*, Charles Lam Markmann, tr., (New York, Random House, 1968), 23–24.

60. Thieck, "La journée," 238.

61. Personal interview with Sharif Hatata, February 28, 1980, Cairo.

62. al-Bishri, *al-Haraka al-siyasiyya*, 100–1.

63. Thieck, "La journée," 209.

64. Personal interview with Fakhri Labib Hanna, December 21, 1979, Cairo.

65. al-Shafii, *Tatawwur*, 79.

66. Jacques Berque, *Egypt: Imperialism and Revolution*, Jean Stewart, tr., (London, Faber, 1972), 579.

67. Thieck, "La journée," 220.

68. See E. P. Thompson, "The Moral Economy of the English Crowd in the Eighteenth Century," *Past and Present* 50 (February 1971): 76–131, for a discussion of crowd behavior.

69. *Egyptian Gazette,* July 12, 1946.

70. Civil Court, Case no. 1949, Abdin, year 1947, 942.

71. Ibid., 730–35.

4 – Unification and Division in the Communist Movement, 1947–1954

1. Iskra was also called al-Talia al-Mutahida after a merger took place between the organization and the People's Liberation.

2. al-Said, *Tarikh al-munazzamat,* 389.

3. FO 371/69250 J1890/1261/16, March 10, 1948. Great Britain, Public Records Office.

4. Henri Curiel, "Les principales étapes du la lutte intériere," 1955, (photocopy).

5. FO 141/1272 176/10/48, April 1, 1948. Great Britain, Public Records Office.

6. Civil Court, Case no. 4872, Azbakiyya, 256, year 1951, 940 (in Arabic).

7. FO 371/630/46 J3595/422/16, July 26, 1947. Great Britain, Public Records Office.

8. FO 141/1158 20/2/24, July 15, 1947. Great Britain, Public Records Office.

9. High Military Court, Case no. 80, al-Darb al-Ahmar, 264, year 1954, 939 (in Arabic).

10. FO 371/69250 J1890/1262/16, March 10, 1948. Great Britain, Public Records Office.

11. FO 371 69250 J2953/1261/16, April 25, 1948. Great Britain, Public Records Office.

12. al-Bishri, *al-Haraka al-siyasiyya,* 423.

13. FO 371/62994 J58/13/16, November 22, 1947. Great Britain, Public Records Office.

14. Personal interview with Ahmad Hamrush, April 11, 1980, Cairo.

15. Ibid.

16. Personal interviews with Albert Arie, April 17, 1980, Cairo, and Hamdi Abd al-Jawab, May 10, 1980, Cairo.

17. Personal interview with Sharif Hatata, February 28, 1980, Cairo.

18. Personal interview with Albert Arie, April 23, 1980, Cairo.

19. Personal interviews with Hamdi Abd al-Jawab, May 10, 1980, and Sharif Hatata, May 4, 1980, Cairo.

20. High Military Court, Case no. 80, al-Darb al-Ahmar, 264, year 1954, 966–87.

21. Personal interview with Sharif Hatata, May 4, 1980, Cairo.

22. Ibid.

23. Ibid.

24. Civil Court, Case no. unavailable, Mansura, year 1949, 46–94 (in Arabic).

25. Ibid.

26. Ibid., 306–8.

27. Personal interview with Ahmad Taha, February 28, 1980, Cairo.

28. al-Bishri, *al-Haraka al-siyasiyya,* 439–40.

29. *al-Misri,* January 12, 1951.

30. Personal interview with Inge Aflatun, January 18, 1980, Cairo.

31. *al-Katib*, May 26, 1951.

32. Personal interview with Inge Aflatun, January 18, 1980, Cairo.

33. Personal interview with Sharif Hatata, February 28, 1980, Cairo.

34. Walter Z. Laqueur, *The Soviet Union and the Middle East* (New York, Praeger, 1959), 146.

35. Fayez Abu Jaber, "Soviet Arab Relations," *Middle East Forum*, vol. 45, no. 1 (1969), 14.

36. al-Bishri, *al-Haraka al-siyasiyya*, 262; al-Said, *Tarikh al-munazzamat*, 192; *al-Jamahir*, May 5, and May 26, 1947.

37. Abdel-Malek, *Egypt*, 28.

38. Personal interview with Albert Arie, April 12, 1980, Cairo.

39. Agwani, *Communism*, 45.

40. The Jewish presence in the DMNL continued until 1950 when, after their release from prison, Curiel and Schwartz were expelled from the country by the government. From this time forward, the DMNL's entire central committee was composed of Egyptians of Muslim origin. Schwartz, it appears, severed his connections with Egyptian communism after his arrival in France. Curiel, on the other hand, gathered around him in Paris a group of Egyptian ex-patriates whose interest in the political affairs of Egypt remained firm, and in a short time he set up *Majmuat Roma* (The Rome Group) — the code name for what developed into his exiled organization. *Majmuat Roma* and the DMNL maintained close ties for the first few years after Curiel's expulsion from Egypt. The Egyptian communists in Paris sent reports to Egypt which dealt with topics of theoretical and practical interest, they helped the DMNL translate and publish material, and they established connections with international communists. *Majmuat Roma* certainly did not run the party, but it worked alongside it whenever possible.

41. al-Bishri, *al-Haraka al-siyasiyya*, 261.

42. *al-Jamahir*, November 22, 1947.

43. Ibid., December 21, 1947.

44. Shudhi Atiya al-Shafii and Abd al-Maabud al-Jibayli, *Ahdafna al-wataniyya*, (Cairo, n.d.), 36–38.

45. RG 319, 245346, October 12, 1948. U.S. National Archives and Records Service.

46. Henri Curiel, *Pour une Paix Juste au Proche Orient* (Paris, Association Henri Curiel, 1979), 12.

47. Lacouture, *Egypt*, 102; Shah Abdul Qayyum, *Egypt Reborn: A Study of Egypt's Freedom Movement, 1945–1952* (New Dehli, S. Chand, 1973), 87.

48. Personal interviews with Muhammad Sid Ahmad, December 24, 1979, and February 16, 1980, Cairo.

49. Personal interview with Ismail Sabri Abd Allah, December 26, 1979, Cairo.

50. Directive entitled, "Un 'cours' sur le front," Democratic Movement for National Liberation, 1954.

51. Personal interview with Ahmad Taha, April 11, 1980, Cairo.

52. Directive entitled, "Le F.D. est la chainon indispensable qui nous ermettra constituer le Parti," Democratic Movement for National Liberation, n.d.

53. Directive entitled, "Le front demoqratique," Democratic Movement for National Liberation, 1950.

54. *al-Malayin*, October 21, 1951.

55. Personal interview with Sharif Hatata, February 28, 1980, Cairo.

56. al-Bishri, *al-Haraka al-siyasiyya*, 434.

57. RG 84 150, August 30, 1948. U.S. National Archives and Records Service.

58. Personal interview with Muhammad Sid Ahmad, December 24, 1979, Cairo.

59. For details about these groups see my dissertation, "Oppositional Politics in Egypt: The Communist Movement, 1936–1954," Harvard University, 1984.

60. Civil Court, Case no. 4872, Azbakiyya, 256, year 1951, 562.

61. Personal interview with Muhammad Sid Ahmad, December 24, 1979, Cairo.

62. Ibid.

63. Ibid.

64. al-Said, *Tarikh al-munazzamat*, 446.

65. Personal interview with Muhammad Sid Ahmad, December 24, 1979, Cairo.

66. Sidney and Odette Solomon left Egypt in the early 1950s and took up residence in France.

67. Roger Louis, *The British Empire in the Middle East, 1945–1951* (London, Oxford University Press, 1984), 736.

68. Personal interview with Ahmad Hamrush, April 13, 1980, Cairo.

69. al-Shafii, *al-Tatawwur*, 114.

70. Mahmoud Hussein, *Class Conflict in Egypt, 1945–1970*, Michel and Susanne Chirman, Alfred Ehrenfeld, and Kathy Brown, trs., (New York, Monthly Review Press, 1977), 71.

71. Personal interview with Sharif Hatata, February 28, 1980, Cairo.

72. Personal interview with Albert Arie, April 3, 1980, Cairo.

73. A position appointed by the government.

74. Personal interview with Ismail Sabri Abd Allah, December 26, 1979, Cairo.

75. Ibid.

76. Ibid.

77. Marie-Dominique Gresh, "Le P.C.F. et L' Égypte: 1950–1956," Mémoire de Maîtrise, Université de Paris I, 1976–1977, 79–80.

78. Personal interview with Fuad Mursi, November 12, 1979, Cairo.

79. Ibid.

80. Ibid.

81. Personal interview with Daud Aziz, January 2, 1980, Cairo.

82. al-Bishri, *al-Haraka al-siyasiyya*, 445.

83. Personal interview with Ismail Sabri Abd Allah, December 26, 1979, Cairo.

84. Personal interview with Daud Aziz, January 2, 1980, Cairo.

85. Salah Isa's interview with Saad Zahran, August 17, 1975, Cairo, transcript of the meeting provided to the author.

86. al-Bishri, *al-Haraka al-siyasiyya*, 452.

87. Personal interview with Daud Aziz, January 2, 1980, Cairo.

88. Personal interview with Ismail Sabri Abd Allah, December 26, 1979, Cairo.

89. Personal interview with Fuad Mursi, December 27, 1979, Cairo.

5 — Communism and the Military Regime

1. Agwani, *Communism*, 48.

2. Personal interview with Muhammad Yusuf al-Jindi, January 27, 1980, Cairo.

3. Personal interview with Khalid Muhyi al-Din, April 2, 1980, Cairo.

4. Personal interview with Ahmad Hamrush, April 11, 1980, Cairo.

5. Personal interview with Khalid Muhyi al-Din, April 2, 1980, Cairo.

6. Ibid.

7. Personal interview with Ahmad Hamrush, April 11, 1980, Cairo.

8. Ibid.

9. Personal interview with Khalid Muhyi al-Din, March 26, 1980, Cairo.

10. Ibid.

11. Ibid.

12. Ibid.

13. Personal interview with Ahmad Hamrush, April 11, 1980, Cairo.

14. Ibid.

15. Ibid.; personal interview with Rifaat al-Said, December 30, 1979, Cairo.

16. Ibid.

17. "Deux Analyses—Deux Politiques la situation actualle en Égypte" in Gresh, "Le P.C.F. et L' Égypte," Vol. 2, 50–72.

18. Personal interview with Fuad Mursi, November 12, 1979, Cairo.

19. Personal interview with Ismail Sabri Abd Allah, December 26, 1979, Cairo.

20. Maxime Rodinson, *Marxism and the Muslim World* (London, Zed, 1979), 163–64.

21. Personal interview with Hilmi Yassin, January 22, 1980, Cairo.

22. Personal interview with Muhammad Mitwali al-Shaarawi, April 15, 1980, Cairo.

23. Lacouture, *Egypt*, 165.

24. "Bulletin d-Études," no. 18, Septembre, 1952, in Gresh, "Le P.C.F. et L' Égypte," Vol. 2, 23.

25. Personal interview with Khalid Muhyi al-Din, April 6, 1980, Cairo.

26. *al-Ahram*, August 14, 1952.

27. Personal interview with Muhammad Mitwali al-Shaarawi, April 15, 1980, Cairo.

28. "Bulletin d' Études," no. 18, Septembre, 1952, in Gresh, "Le P.C.F. et L' Égypte," Vol. 2, 23.

29. Personal interview with Khalid Muhyi al-Din, April 6, 1980, Cairo.

30. Ibid.

31. Personal interview with Fuad Mursi, December 27, 1979, Cairo.

32. Personal interview with Hilmi Yassin, January 22, 1980, Cairo.

33. Personal interview with Muhammad Yusuf al-Jindi, January 27, 1980, Cairo.

34. Personal interview with Muhammad Mitwali al-Shaarawi, April 15, 1980, Cairo.

35. Personal interview with Ahmad Taha, February 25, 1980, Cairo.

36. Rodinson, *Marxism*, 169–70.

37. The Muslim Brotherhood was considered an organization, not a political party. It too was banned a year later when it challenged the military's rule.

38. Hrair Dekmejian, *Egypt under Nasir*, (Albany, State University of New York), 25.

39. High Military Court, Case no. 80 al-Darb al-Ahmar, 264, year 1954, 322.

40. "Appel de la ligue des étudiants du M.D.L.N. a tous les étudiants Égyptiens," in Gresh, "Le P.C.F. et L' Égypte," Vol. 2, 37–41.

41. High Military Court, Case no. 80, al-Darb al-Ahmar, 264, year 1954, 659–60.

42. Ibid., 81–82.

43. Ibid., 83, 303–4.

44. Ibid., 672.
45. Ibid., 652–54.
46. Personal interview with Khalid Muhyi al-Din, April 6, 1980, Cairo.
47. Eliezer Beeri, *Army Officers in Arab Politics and Society* (New York, Praeger, 1970), 114–15.
48. Lacouture, *Egypt,* 182–83.
49. Ibid., 183.
50. Personal interview with Khalid Muhyi al-Din, March 26, 1980, Cairo.
51. Ibid., April 6, 1980.
52. Ibid.
53. Personal interview with Muhammad Sid Ahmad, July 18, 1986, Cairo.
54. Personal interview with Fuad Mursi, July 14, 1986, Cairo.
55. Personal interview with Sharif Hatata, July 20, 1986, Cairo.
56. Personal interview with Muhammad Sid Ahmad, July 31, 1986, Cairo.
57. Ibid., July 18, 1986.
58. Personal interview with Fuad Mursi, July 14, 1986, Cairo.
59. Ibid., July 20, 1986.

6 – The Significance of the Egyptian Communist Movement

1. Personal interview with Muhammad Sid Ahmad, December 24, 1979, Cairo.
2. Ibid.

Appendix – Journalistic Literature

1. Personal interview with Muhammad Sid Ahmad, December 24, 1979, Cairo.
2. For more information see Rifaat al-Said, *al-Sihafa al-yasariyya fi misr, 1925–1948* (Cairo, 1977), and *al-Sihafa al-yasariyya fi misr, 1950–1952* (Beirut, 1981).
3. Personal interview with Louis Awad, April 22, 1980, Cairo.
4. Personal interview with Anwar Kamil, April 27, 1980, Cairo.
5. Personal interview with Louis Awad, April 22, 1979, Cairo.
6. Thieck, "La journée," 161.
7. RG 319 287807, June 13, 1946. U.S. National Archives and Records Service.

Bibliography

Unpublished Materials

Government Documents

Egypt. Mahfuzat Majlis al-Wuzara, Wizarat al-Dakhiliyya in the Dar al-Wathaiq, Cairo, "Taqarir al-Amn." Reports from the Special Branch, Cairo Police to the Ministry of the Interior, 1940 and 1941 (in Arabic).

France. Archives of the French Embassy in Cairo.

Great Britain. Foreign Office Archives in the Public Records Office, London; FO 141, 371.

United States. National Archives and Records Service, Washington, D.C.; RG 84, 85, 319.

Court Cases

Judicial Inquiry of Anwar Kamil before the High Military Prosecutor in the Case of Socialism and the Bread and Freedom group, Cairo, 1942 (in Arabic).

Civil Court, Case no. 1949, Abdin, year 1947 (in Arabic).

Civil Court, Case no. unavailable, Mansura, year 1949 (in Arabic).

Civil Court, Case no. 2021, Misr Qadima, 247, year 1951 (in Arabic).

Civil Court, Case no. 4872, Azbakiyya, 256, year 1951 (in Arabic).

Civil Court, Case no. 287, Shubra, year 1953 (in Arabic).

High Military Court, Case no. 80, al-Darb al-Ahmar, 264, year 1954 (in Arabic).

High Military Court, Case no. 150, year 1956 (in Arabic).

Private Papers

Relating to the Egyptian Communist Movement from: the Archives of the Egyptian Movement for National Liberation and the Democratic Movement of National Liberation; Salah Isa; Rifaat al-Said; Yusuf Darwish. Relating to women in radical Egyptian politics from: Inge Aflatun.

Interviews

Ismail Sabri Abd Allah
Enayet Adham
Soraya Adham
Inge Aflatun
Muhammad Sid Ahmad
Albert Arie
Louis Awad
Daud Aziz
Aime Beresi
Muhammad Fakri
Muhammad Hasan Gad
Jamal Ghali
Fuad Habashi
Tahir Abd al-Hakim
Ahmad Hamrush
Fakhri Labib Hanna
Shahata Harun
Sharif Hatata
Joseph Hazan

Hamdi Abd al-Jawab
Muhammad Yusuf al-Jindi
Adli Jirjis
Fawzi Jirjis
Anwar Kamil
Sayyid Khayyal
Lutfi al-Kholi
Khalid Muhyi al-Din
Fuad Mursi
Rifaat al-Said
Muhammad Mitwali al-Shaarawi
Raymond Stambouli
Lutfallah Sulayman
Ahmad Taha
Mustafa Tiba
Hilmi Yassin
Latifa al-Zayat
Suad Zuhayr

Unpublished Theses

Ashmawi, al-Sayyid Muhammad. "Tarikh al-fikr al-siyasi al-misri, 1945–1952." Ph.D. Thesis, Cairo University, 1977.

Beinin, Joel. "Class Conflict and National Struggle: Labor and Politics in Egypt, 1936–1954." Ph.D. Thesis University of Michigan, 1982.

Cantori, Louis Joseph. "The Organizational Basis of an Elite Political Party: The Wafd." Ph.D. Thesis, University of Chicago, 1966.

Gresh, Marie-Dominique. "Le P.C.F. et L' Égypte: 1950–1956." Mémoire de Maîtrise, Université de Paris I, 1976–1977.

Hammam, Mona. "Women Workers and the Practice of Freedom as Education: The Egyptian Experience." Ph.D. Thesis, University of Kansas, 1977.

Ismail, Mahmoud. "Nationalism in Egypt Before Nasser's Revolution." Ph.D. Thesis, University of Pittsburgh, 1966.

Lockman, Zachary. "Class and Nation: The Emergence of the Egyptian Workers' Movement." Ph.D. Thesis, Harvard University, 1983.

Thieck, Jean-Pierre. "La journée du 21 Février 1946 dans l'histoire du mouvement national Égyptien." Diplôme d'études superieures en histoire, Université de Paris VIII, 1974.

Published Materials

Newspapers and Periodicals

(*in Arabic*)
>   al-Ahd al-Jadid (1944–1945)
>   al-Ahram
>   al-Bashir (1950)
>   al-Damir (1945–1946)
>   al-Fajr al-Jadid (1945–1946)
>   Hurriyat al-Shuub (1946–1952)
>   al-Jamahir (1947–1948)
>   al-Katib (1951)
>   al-Kutla
>   al-Majalla al-Jadida
>   al-Malayin (1951)
>   al-Misri
>   al-Muarada (1952)
>   al-Mustaqbal (1950)
>   al-Nas (1951)
>   Rabitat al-Shabab (1945–1946)
>   al-Talia (1945–1946)
>   al-Tatawwur (1940)
>   Umdurman (1945–1946)
>   al-Wajib (1952)

(*in English*)
>   Egyptian Gazette
>   Labour Monthly

Books and Articles in Arabic

Abbas, Rauf. *al-Haraka al-ummaliyya fi misr, 1899–1952*. Cairo, 1967.

Ahdafna. Rabitat Fatayat al-Jamia wa al-Maahid al-Misriyya (League of Women Students and Graduates from the University and Egyptian Institutes). Cairo, 1946.

Ahmad, Muhammad Hasan. *al-Ikhwan al-muslimun fi al-mizan*. Cairo, 1946.

Aflatun, Inge. *80 Malyun imraa maana*. Cairo, 1948.

———. *Nahnu al-nisa al-misriyyat*. Cairo, 1949.

———. *al-Salam wa al-jala*. Cairo, 1950.

Anis, Muhammad. *Arbaa Fibrayir 1942 fi tarikh misr al-siyasi*. Beirut, 1972.

Awad, Louis. *al-Anqa au tarikh Hasan al-Muftah*. Beirut, 1966.

———. "Dikrayat Baida," in *Hommage á Georges Henein*. Le Caire, Le Part du Sable, 1974.

al-Bishri, Tariq. *al-Haraka al-siyasiyya fi misr, 1945–1952*. Cairo, 1972.

Dirasat min Dar al-Abhath al-Ilmiyya. Cairo, 1945/1946.

al-Disuqi, Asim Ahmad. *Kibar mullak al-aradi al-ziraiyya wa dawruhum fi al-mujtama al-misri, 1914–1952*. Cairo, 1975.

al-Ghazzali, Abd al-Munim. *Tarikh al-haraka al-niqabiyya al-misriyya, 1899–1952*. Cairo, 1968.

Halim, Asad. *Misr baada ilan al-harb*. Cairo, 1945.

Hamrush, Ahmad. *Qissat thawrat 23 yulyu*. Vol. 4. Beirut, 1977.

Izz al-Din, Amin. *Tarikh al-tabaqa al-amila al-misriyya, 1919–1939*. Cairo, 1972.

Jirjis, Fawzi. *Dirasat fi tarikh misr al-siyasi mundhu asr al-mamalik*. Cairo, 1958.

Kamil, Anwar. *Afyun al-Shaab*. Cairo, 1948.

———. *La tabaqat*. Cairo, 1945.

al-Masilhi, Hasan. *Qissati maa al-shuyuiyya*. Cairo, 1979.

Musa, Salama. *al-Ishtirakiyya*. Cairo, 1962.

Mutawalli, Mahmud. *Misr wa al-haraka al-shuyuiyya khilal al-harb al-alamiyya al-thaniyya*. Cairo, 1979.

al-Nukhayli, Sulayman. *Tarikh al-haraka al-ummaliyya fi misr*. Cairo, 1963.

Ramadan, Abd al-Azim. *Abd al-Nasir wa azmat Maris*. Cairo, 1976.

———. *Tatawwur al-haraka al-wataniyya al-misriyya, 1917–1936*. Cairo, 1968.

———. *Tatawwur al-haraka al-wataniyya fi misr min sanat 1937 ila sana 1948*. 2 vols. Beirut, n.d.

Rifai, Abd al-Aziz. *al-Ummal wa al-haraka al-qawmiyya fi misr al-haditha, 1900–1952*. Cairo, n.d.

Saad, Ahmad Sadiq. *Filastin baina makhalib al-istimar*. Cairo, 1945/46.

———. *Mushkilat al-falah*. Cairo, 1945.

———. *Safahat min al-yasar al-misri*. Cairo, 1976.

al-Said, Rifaat. *al-Sihafa al-yasariyya fi misr, 1925–1948*. Cairo, 1977.

———. *al-Sihafa al-yasariyya fi misr, 1950–1952*. Beirut, 1981.

———. *Tarikh al-haraka al-ishtirakiyya fi misr, 1900–1925*. Cairo, 1975.

———. *Tarikh al-munazzamat al-yasariyya al-misriyya, 1940–1950*. Cairo, 1976.

———. *al-Yasar al-misri, 1925–1940*. Beirut, 1972.

———. *al-Yasar al-misri wa al-qadiya al-filastiniyya*. Beirut, 1974.

Salih, Ahmad Rushdi. *Cromir fi misr*. Cairo, 1945.

al-Shafii, Shuhdi Atiya. *Tatawwur al-haraka al-wataniyya al-misriyya, 1882–1956*. Cairo, 1956.

al-Shafii, Shuhdi Atiya and Abd al-Maabud al-Jibayli. *Ahdafna al-wataniyya*. Cairo, n.d.

Uthman, Taha Saad. "Mudhakkirat wa watha'iq min tarikh al-tabaqa al-amila." *al-Katib* 11 (July 1971) to 12 (July 1972).

Books and Articles in English and French

Abdalla, Ahmed. *The Student Movement and National Politics in Egypt*, London, Al Saqi Books, 1985.

Abdel-Malek, Anouar. *Egypt: Military Society, the Army Regime, the Left, and Social Change under Nasser*, Charles Lam Markmann, tr., New York, Random House, 1968.

Abou Alam, Abdel Raouf. *The Labor Movement in Egypt*, Washington D.C., Egyptian Embassy, 1955.

Abu Jaber, Fayez. "Soviet Arab Relations," *Middle East Forum*, vol. 45, no. 1 (1969).

Agwani, M. S. *Communism in the Arab East*, New York, Asia Publishing House, 1969.

Audsley, M. T. "Labour and Social Affairs in Egypt." *St. Antony's Papers* 4 (1958).

al-Barawi, Rashed. *Economic Development in the U.A.R.*, Cairo, Anglo-Egyptian Bookshop, 1970.

———. *The Military Coup in Egypt*, Cairo, Renaissance Publishers, 1952.

Bardell, Samuel. *A Note on the Funeral of Henri Curiel*, May, 1978.

Batatu, Hanna. *The Old Social Classes and the Revolutionary Movements of Iraq*, Princeton, Princeton University Press, 1978.

Beeri, Eliezer. *Army Officers in Arab Politics and Society*, New York, Praeger, 1970.

Berque, Jacques. *Egypt: Imperialism and Revolution*. Jean Stewart, tr., London, Faber, 1972.

Bulletin Henri Curiel. Paris, Association Henri Curiel, No. 2, décembre, 1978; no. 5, juin, 1979; Special, septembre, 1979; no. 7, mars, 1980.

Colombe, Marcel. *L'Evolution de L'Égypte, 1924–1940*, Paris, Maisonneuve, 1951.

Curiel, Henri. *Pages Auto-Biographiques*, Digne, Association Henri Curiel, 1977.

———. *Pour une paix juste au Proche Orient*, Paris, Association Henri Curiel, 1979.

———. "Les principales etapes du la lutte interiere," 1955, (xerox).

Deeb, Marius. *Party Politics in Egypt: The Wafd and Its Rivals, 1919–1939*, London, Ithaca Press, 1979.

DeGras, Jane. *The Communist International, 1919–1943*, London, F. Cass, 1971.

Dekmejian, Hrair. *Egypt Under Nasir*, Albany, State University of New York, 1971.

Gibb, H. A. R. "Middle East Perplexities." *International Affairs* 20, 4 (October 1944).

Gran, Peter. "Modern Trends in Egyptian Historiography: A Review Article." *International Journal of Middle Eastern Studies* 9, 3 (August 1978).

Groves, J. C. *The Arab Attitude to Communism with Special Reference to*

Nasser's Egypt, Geneve, Institut universitaire de hautes études internationales, 1963.

Hansen, Bent and Marzouk, Girgis A. *Development and Economic Policy in the UAR (Egypt)*, Amsterdam, North-Holland Publishing Co., 1965.

Hatata, Sharif. *The Eye with an Iron Lid*, London, Onyx Press, 1982.

Hourani, Albert. *Arabic Thought in the Liberal Age*, London, Oxford University Press, 1970.

———. *Minorities in the Arab World*, London, Oxford University Press, 1947.

Hussein, Mahmoud. *Class Conflict in Egypt, 1945–1970*, Michel and Susanne Chirman, Alfred Ehrenfeld, and Kathy Brown, trs., New York, Monthly Review Press, 1977.

Israel, Marcel. "Esquisse Historique Mouvement Communiste Égyptien," Report presented to the Italian Communist Party, n.d. (xerox).

Issawi, Charles. *Egypt: An Economic and Social Analysis*, London, Oxford University Press, 1947.

———. *Egypt at Mid-Century*, London, Oxford University Press, 1954.

———. *Egypt in Revolution: An Economic Analysis*, London, Oxford University Press, 1963.

Jankowski, James. *Egypt's Young Rebels: "Young Egypt," 1933–1952*, Stanford, Hoover Institute Press, 1975.

Kautsky, John H. *Communism and the Politics of Development*, New York, Wiley, 1968.

el-Kosheri Mahfouz, Afaf. *Socialisme et Pouvoir en Égypte*, Paris, Librairie general de droit et de jurisprudence, 1972.

Lacouture, Jean and Simmone. *Egypt in Transition*, New York, Criterion Books, 1958.

Landshut, Siegfried. *Jewish Communities in the Muslim Countries of the Middle East*, London, Jewish Chronicle, 1950.

Laqueur, Walter Z. *Communism and Nationalism in the Middle East*, London, Routledge and Kegan Paul, 1956.

———. *The Soviet Union and the Middle East*, New York, Praeger, 1959.

Louis, Roger. *The British Empire in the Middle East, 1945–1951*, London, Oxford University Press, 1984.

Makarious, Raoul. *La Jeunesse Intellectuale d'Égypte au Lendemain de la Deuxième Guerre Mondiale*, Paris, Mouton, 1960.

Marsot, Afaf Lutfi al-Sayyid. "The Revolutionary Gentlewomen in Egypt," in Lois Beck and Nikki Keddie, eds., *Women in the Muslim World*, Cambridge, Mass., Harvard University Press, 1978.

Mitchell, Richard P. *The Society of Muslim Brothers*, London, Oxford University Press, 1969.

Moore, Austin. *Farewell Farouk*, Chicago, Scholars' Press, 1954.

Musa, Salama. *The Education of Salama Musa*, Leiden, Brill, 1961.

Naguib, Mohammad. *Egypt's Destiny*, London, Gollancz, 1955.

Perrault, Gilles. *Un homme à part*, Paris, B. Barrault, 1984.

Qayyum, Shah Abdul. *Egypt Reborn: A Study of Egypt's Freedom Movement, 1945–1952*, New Dehli, S. Chand, 1973.

Rodinson, Maxime. *Marxism and the Muslim World*, London, Zed, 1979.

Safran, Nadav. *Egypt in Search of Political Community*, Cambridge, Mass., Harvard University Press, 1961.

Sanson, A. W. *I Spied Spies*, London, Harrap, 1965.

Sworakowski, Witold S. *World Communism*, Stanford, Hoover Institute Press, 1973.

Thompson, E. P. "The Moral Economy of the English Crowd in the Eighteenth Century." *Past and Present* 50 (February 1971).

Vatikiotis, P. J. *The Modern History of Egypt*, London, Weidenfeld and Nicolson, 1969.

Wayment, Hilary, ed. *Egypt Now*, Cairo, Le Groupe Études, 1942.

Index

183